James Douglas Jerrold Kelley

A Desperate Chance, a Story of Land and Sea

James Douglas Jerrold Kelley

A Desperate Chance, a Story of Land and Sea

ISBN/EAN: 9783744718356

Printed in Europe, USA, Canada, Australia, Japan

Cover: Foto ©Andreas Hilbeck / pixelio.de

More available books at **www.hansebooks.com**

A DESPERATE CHANCE

A STORY OF LAND AND SEA

BY

J. D. JERROLD KELLEY

COMMANDER, U. S. N.

CONTENTS.

	PAGE
CHAPTER I.	
DALTON'S JOURNAL, ...	1
CHAPTER II.	
RUE ST. PIERRE, ...	21
CHAPTER III.	
THE COLONEL'S STORY, ...	37
CHAPTER IV.	
ISABEL, ...	59
CHAPTER V.	
A QUEER LOT, ...	75
CHAPTER VI.	
GIBRALTAR, ...	106
CHAPTER VII.	
HALCYON AHOY!	125
CHAPTER VIII.	
HOMEWARD BOUND, ...	144

CONTENTS.

CHAPTER IX.
A Dark Night, ... 167

CHAPTER X.
Stout Hearts, ... 198

CHAPTER XI.
Dawn, ... 216

CHAPTER XII.
Daylight, ... 225

A DESPERATE CHANCE.

CHAPTER I.

From the journal of John Brewerton Dalton, a Surgeon in the United States Navy.

Flagship Columbia,
Off Toulon, France, *5th March,* *1879.*

THE band of the Infanterie de Marine had just finished the programme of the evening, and the soldiers were removing the music stands and portable lights from the Square, when I saw coming toward me the woman who had been watching us from a corner of the Place d'armes. She moved irresolutely, and as the crowd swept noisily into a narrow street, I lost sight of her from my seat in front of the Restaurant Jean Bart, where I had been dining with Hippolyte Delmonte, the senior medical officer of the convict station.

I thought no more of her, after this, as my

mind was already disturbed by an incident which had interrupted our dinner. For some days Delmonte and I had been deeply interested in a convict who was the only Englishman then undergoing punishment, and as we were taking our coffee, news had come of his attempted suicide. The man had been sent to the hospital soon after his arrival in Toulon, and from the beginning had, under adverse circumstances, displayed so many unexpected qualities, that the interest and sympathy of the physicians were excited in his favor. I had spoken to him several times offering such services as the rules permitted, but he had always answered quietly, never complaining of his misery nor making any requests, until my last visit when he said:

"Thank you, Doctor Dalton, there is one favor which I can ask, because, though a convict, I am not, in the higher sense, nor morally, a criminal. It is this. Should I die in this rat hole, try and bury me where God's free air may come, and let some tender English prayer be said in memory of what I have been."

He was so much a mystery to both of us, that we were again discussing the probable history of 2008—such was his prison individuality—when an orderly approached hurriedly and gave Delmonte a note.

He opened it leisurely, but in a moment his face filled with sorrow, and he said:

"Hein, Dalton! our mystery will be unsolved forever, if not revealed within an hour. Your countryman is dying."

"My countryman?" I asked, with a nervous premonition of some unknown evil.

"Yes! Our Englishman, 2008, proves to be an American; he has taken poison, procured no one knows how, and of such potency that he cannot live; at least so says the assistant who writes this—I must leave you."

"Can I be of service?" I asked.

"Perhaps." Then he added, "At what time do you go on board ship?"

"In the eleven o'clock boat, which leaves the inner landing by the police ship."

"And until that hour?" he inquired.

"I shall stay here and finish my cigar."

"Well, if I need you, I shall send here or to the landing stage. Is your aumonier—how do you call him—your chaplain—is he ashore?"

"Yes; he came with me, before sundown."

"Can he be found at this hour?—for the dying man may need him. A poor ending this, for any one, Dalton, but doubly sad for such as our convict, as I am sure, he was a gentleman."

Delmonte walked quickly under the trees

towards the avenue leading to the Arsenal Gate, but in the shadow, where the street makes a half turn by the walls of the Préfet's garden, the woman I had noticed before, stopped him with a nervous entreaty. He bowed courteously, made some reply to her questioning and, calling a passing quarter-master of the fleet, pointed me out; then, with another salute, he hurried upon his errand of mercy.

The woman hesitated, drawing back into the shadow of the trees, and I lost sight of her in the crowd which followed the band and its escort.

A quiet place is the Place d'armes at night, when the music is finished, and now it was almost deserted save by a few loungers like myself, and by the sentries whose muskets gleamed in the gaslight, and whose measured tread awoke disturbing echoes on the pavement in front of the official residence. Clouds were gathering overhead, and the southerly breeze sighed in the topmost branches of the poplars.

"Time to be going," I thought, looking at my watch, and feeling the loneliness of the place; "and yet I should like to know how that poor fellow makes his struggle for life. Dead, perhaps, and in such a place. Heaven pity him!"

The half hour struck faintly from a distant clock; a great bell tolled solemnly; there was a bugle-call from somewhere, strange too, at that hour; and, in the heart of the town, dogs were baying; from the harbor came the quick ringing of five bells on the men-of-war, and the hails of the watchful sentries punctuated the night with a sudden, sharp distinctness which made oppressive the silence that followed.

I tossed off the last of the demi-tasse, puffed my cigar into a friendly blaze, and arose to go, when I again saw the woman stealing out of the gloom. She seemed afraid to leave a shadow on the pavement or to awake an echo that might reveal her hiding-place; for she walked, not in the open pathway, but cat-like in the dusk of the angles; at last reaching the one nearest to me, she halted, cut off by its screen from the flooding light of the café.

It was the woman I had seen before and lost, and who was now, as if by a determined effort, about to address me. I saluted her courteously, placed a chair where the shadow of a tree would in some degree hide her from the passers-by, and awaited her pleasure.

In a low, quick voice, that was hard and metallic with suppressed emotion, and in perfect English, she said,

"Pardon me, Dr. Dalton?"

"At your service, Madame," I replied. For a

second I had hesitated over this last word, but I saw she was not in that debatable land where the term may be offensive or most proper, as circumstances demand.

"Surgeon in the American Navy, and of the Frigate Columbia?" she asked me, quickly.

"I am Dr. Dalton, a surgeon in the navy, and attached to the ship you have named."

"Pardon me again. But"—and here she paused for a moment as if to be certain of her phrase—"I doubted the correctness of my information, as you are not—like these others, these French—you are not in uniform."

"Dr. Delmonte informed you?" I inquired.

"Dr. Delmonte?" she repeated. "Ah, yes! The officer in naval uniform who left your table, and who is, so I am informed, the physician of the Prison Hospital. The Bagne, I believe it is called."

"Dr. Delmonte," I answered, "is chief-of-staff of the Bagne."

She drew her chair out of the shadow, and after a moment of hesitation, but in the same low voice which betrayed little of the misery that must have been crushing her, said:

"Oh, sir! I am your countrywoman and friendless. Can you not aid me? I arrived but an hour since, and must go at once to the Hospital of the Convict Station."

So, she had come from the north, as the southern trains are earlier and later. Evidently no gamester this, stranded on the reefs of Monte Carlo. I waited, as she watched me with burning eyes, and replied, quietly,—

"What you ask is, I regret to say, impossible."

"Impossible? Oh, do not say that!" she interrupted, with eager and pitiful entreaty.

"At this hour," I added, "all the gates are, by regulations, closed, and the code of the administration is most rigid."

"But," she pleaded, "mercy will relax that code, pity will soften that administration. Your companion, Dr. Delmonte, said the same. I told him of my necessity, but in vain. Then I begged as a helpless foreigner, an American—and here he interrupted me and declared that a matter of life and death depended upon his haste. He gave me your name and station, and pointed you out as one who would inform me what his necessities forbade. Will you not help me?" she entreated, tearfully; "I appeal to you as a friendless woman to a gentleman, as a countrywoman alone in a strange land to her countryman, as a sufferer to a physician."

She paused, overmastered by emotion, and then continued: "I must go to the hospital, and, all else failing, by your aid."

What could I do? Though pitying her from my heart, I knew what she asked was impossible. I said to her:

"I am, in this matter, powerless. You would have more right to ask the privilege than I, for my official position forbids. To enter the Dock Yard, a pass from the Commandant is required, and the office of the Rear-Admiral has been closed for many hours. I regret this deeply, but it is a charity to tell you. Forgive my frankness and cruelty, but I must repeat, what you ask is impossible."

"God help and pity me, then!" she cried, and with a low moan like that of a hunted animal, stricken to death in a tangle of brush, she sank helpless upon the chair.

There was the half-caught strain of a jolly song from a distant Brasserie, echoed by a chorus I had heard in the Alcazar, when the house rose to the witcheries of the latest Parisian success; from the café behind me, bubbled the riotous laughter of the domino-players, and at the instant, a woman went by, swaying unsteadily on the arm of a tipsy soldier, who made a silly joke upon the environment.

I fancied I could hear the rising tide lapping the prison walls, and the echoes of the breezes challenging, in their idle liberty, the men who tossed in dreamful slumber on board the galley hulks which darkened the inner harbor. At that time, too, the sentry at the Préfecture came to a salute, and I saw the gallant old Contre-Amiral climbing the steps of the grim house which represented the might of law and government.

I lifted the woman's head, called to the waiter for a carafe of brandy, and dashing it with a midshipman's allowance of water, forced the draught between her lips.

She revived slowly, and as if in pain. "A stern, determined woman, this," I thought, as I looked at the straight brow, the clearly defined angles of the jaws, and the thin lips, revealing teeth, which set closely above a sharply chiselled chin. "A woman to suffer, and in silence; to work in the shadow, and to wait, and, at the end, to grasp success only as a step to some foredetermined victory which the world would mark as hopeless. A woman potent for great good, or greater evil, an individuality which no opposition could defashion of its angles and elemental lines."

She sipped the spirits, and looking at the clouded sky with eyes which gleamed above the hollows of her pale cheeks, demanded in a voice weak with emotion,—

"Pardon my persistence; tell me, where does this Commandant live?"

"In the Arsenal, and at this hour you can see him only by appointment, certified by pass or countersign."

"Who can give this pass, this countersign?"

"I cannot answer. In my night visits, I have been always accompanied by an officer."

"Who, then, is the senior officer? Is there a political, a naval, a military superior, whose authority is paramount?"

"Always," I answered, with some lightness in my tone. "Yes, the Préfet—his word is law."

This seemed to eliminate one factor from the problem with which she had been struggling, for she rose, exultant, transfigured by a new hope, and cried, joyously,

"Come, let us go to him."

In this woman's hands I was helpless, and I found myself reasoning, that the Préfet, though a power in the land, was not the Grand Llama, nor yet the awful Mikado; so I replied:

"He lives opposite, where you see the sentry, and has at this moment returned. As you have asked me, I shall go with you; but how will you explain this desire to enter the hospital?"

"Come, come," she insisted, nervously; "let

us go. My need is great, and I can tell all when I see this Mayor—this Governor—is it?"

"Préfet."

"Thank you, this Préfet. At present," she continued, "we must not hesitate. I have lost too much time already in addressing you, but I feared the crowded square, the people here and around the tables—I feared your generous dinner."

We crossed the dingy old *Place*, and as I was answering the hail of the sentry, I heard the man who had waited at dinner calling loudly. He ran to me and delivered a note just left by a messenger. It was addressed in the quaint, Gallican scrawl of Delmonte, and I read this:

"MY DEAR DALTON: The American is dying and there is no hope. He has asked to see you. Can you come at once? Enclosed is a pass for two, in case the ship's priest should be with you."

I struck out my line of action at once. I knew the chaplain was ashore, philandering theologically with some religious American stopping at the Croix d'Or, en route to Barcelona, so I sent him a line to await further instructions at the Arsenal Gate.

Turning down the narrow street in the rear of the Préfecture, the woman following, I said:

"At the risk of violating a sacred confidence, I can take you to the hospital, but I cannot promise you will accomplish anything."

"I shall not fail, if you will take me there," she replied, in a tone out of which all entreaty had now passed.

"I rely upon your discretion," I continued; "and I hope your necessity, of which I ask no explanation, justifies you placing me in this position."

She bowed her head, declined the arm I felt bound to offer, threw a heavy veil over her face, and, without further words, we walked down the quiet street to the Dock Yard.

We passed the challenging sentries, accompanied by the Sergeant of the Guard, who met us where we were first halted, and going through the Arsenal Gate, after the moment's delay which the viséing of our passes demanded, turned hurriedly toward the avenue, whereon the hospital is situated.

I marked how noiselessly the woman walked, and, as if unconsciously, how she sought always the shadow of the walls and workshops. An unvexed quiet lay upon the place, save for my footsteps ringing loudly upon the pavement, and evoking echoes which followed and went before. There was a sense of space about us, measureless, seemingly, as the skies, and as with eager feet the woman gave the pace which led me, we seemed to be isolated in a deserted land. In the many turnings where buildings uprose with sudden unexpectedness, uncanny spirits seemed to be lurking; and when, after a time, we drew into a wider common, where lights were rare and the pavement ended, my strange companion repelled me as if she were a thing of evil luring to certain woe. She walked with a steadfast purpose and in silence, looking neither to the right nor left, and, as if by intuition, always toward the shining lights of the hospital. When these grew clear, she raised her head, and, as her hands clasped and unclasped each other nervously, she appeared to be preparing for some supreme effort.

We were admitted to the ante-room, and I asked her to wait until I had made my explanations. Learning that Delmonte was in the ward above, I mounted the stairs quietly, and, opening a swinging door, entered the long, white room. A sad place at any time is this refuge of the sick, but at night it is ghostly and drear in the subdued hush and light, though ever and always the only haven of rest, where the convicts find in illness, or in death, a relief from the misery of their hopeless lives.

In a far corner of the room, where a shaded lamp burned dimly, knelt a priest, bending his white head to the lips of a dying man, and listening to that awful recital of repentant guilt, which must be doubly filled with human wickedness when its outcome is in such a place and from such a penitent. Nearer the door a nun was soothing the fevered cheeks of an Algerian convict, who murmured in his restless slumber odd bits of the Koran—queer sentences of hope and fear and trust which had slumbered in his desert-steeped soul, as the half-remembered memories of old home songs sleep till heard alone in foreign lands. But under the outstretched arms of an ivory crucifix in the transept, where the moonlight, streaming through an unshaded window, rested on the crown of the bowed head of the Master, was a bed around which a few silent people were watching the man I had come to see.

2008! What more did we know of him whose name in childhood had run the rosary of a mother's prayers!—what more of him who had been a father's hope and tender care! Convict and felon,—here he was lying, wan, pallid, and breathing away the last of an ill-spent and a self-immolated life; the fair face which the Southern sun had tanned with unpitying beams, looked more homelike in its pallor than ever before;

and in the deep brown eyes turned so hopelessly to mine was a likeness to other eyes I loved in that dear Western land of ours.

Delmonte drew me aside and said, "Nothing can be done; he may die at any moment. Is your chaplain here?"

With some shame, I explained the liberty I had taken with his official permission, and gave my reasons. After a minute's reflection, his face brightened and he said,—

"It is a violation of the rules, without doubt; but humanity must not be crushed by the wheels of discipline. I will assume the responsibility and will send to the Gate for the Chaplain, who should by this time have received your note." When I had thanked him for his consideration, he asked,

"The lady is below? Good! I will talk to her. Graviére, my assistant, is here,—you know him?" As he turned to go where the stricken woman was awaiting, he added, "Ah, Dalton, a sad, sad affair this!"

The dying man soon recognized me, for after looking in the steadfast manner which characterizes the sick, he muttered, feebly,

"Nearly over, doctor, thank God—nearly over. Life has been so hard with me." In a little while he whispered,

"Give me your hand."

I reached my hand out to him and to his misery, and, bending down, asked him to make his peace with God.

"Do you believe God will forgive such as I am and have been," he said, in trembling tones, but not with despair; for, almost immediately, he added, "Ah, yes; I think so. My life has been so sad, and so weary, that He, knowing all, will forgive me."

The feeble hand slipped from mine and the fading eyes turned to where the image of the crucified Saviour, the ever-present symbol of these prayerful ones of another faith, looked down from its soft nimbus of shimmering moonlight.

"He knows," the convict murmured, "He knows;" and the blanched lips trembled with a scarcely perceptible motion of prayer; his fingers played nervously upon the coverlid and then followed spasms, which became less recurrent and less violent as the poisoned life blood yielded to the power of the drug. But in every quiet interval he clasped my hand, and clinging with his soul to our land over the waste of waters, he uttered only one word—"Home."

Our chaplain entered, and the rest withdrew to a little distance, while the words of consolation taught and made sacred by the minister's holy office, were said. The noise of this entrance, subdued though it was, awoke the Arab, who glared at us with a scornful smile upon his lips; but as the lurid eyes of the criminal from the land of the Kabyle turned to the nun, who was kneeling at the bedside of the American, their wickedness died, and into their depths a tenderness crept, as the rift of blue sky blesses the brooding waters where the lightning and the storm have fretted.

The priest came nearer and fell upon his knees; and over all was the hush of the middle night, the awful quiet when God is nearest, and the future trembles on the shores of the present, as the dawn dreams upon the breast of the night. The ticking of a clock made each second seem a minute, and save for this the silence was broken only by the slowly dropping beads of the nun's rosary and by the breathings of the dying man, which rose and fell, as if with amens, to the prayers she was making for him and forever.

An awful quiet. No one moved, and in the hush it seemed as if the world was waiting what would so surely be. Then came the indistinct monotone of a sergeant repeating his night orders to the relief, and when this was stilled, the cadence of the marching men receded and was lost, as echoes die amid the hills.

The quiet of immortality and of peace for death was here.

Suddenly a pallid face looked through the doorway, an eerie, unearthly cry broke upon the night, and the woman I had met in the Toulon streets dashed through the portals and cried,—

"Oh, my love, my Philip, my love, live for me!"

With outstretched arms and yearning eyes, she halted by the doorway, while the face of the dying man flushed as a sunset sea with the tide of ebbing life, and then, with a last effort slowly sought this ghost of his past, uprisen now.

"Home!" he murmured. "Home! God knows best and all."

His hands were lifted in trembling supplication, but not to her; and, with a smile of hope transfiguring his weary face, he turned to the crucifix on the wall, and thus turning, passed away.

For a time no one spoke. We stared affrightedly and unnerved at this ending; all but the sweet sister, whose face rested with infinite love upon the image of the dead Christ, looking down from His symbol of atonement, upon the man He had died to save.

The woman groped her way to the bedside, and in the mad incoherency of grief, poured out a confession of such hopeless, unbounded love, mingled with such threats of revenge upon the unnamed maker of this wreck, that I, who alone understood her, pray heaven I may never hear its like again.

Quietly, and with the benediction of a life's sacrifice upon her, the nun came to her suffering woman, and said,—

"My sister, God is good. He died for such as this is, for such as we are. Pray to Him."

We left them there, Delmonte and I, and with the silvered glory gone from the thorn-encircled brow of the Master; and, as we passed out, we saw them, in the great common humanity of prayer and divine dependence, kneeling there, minister and priest, suffering woman and pale sweet nun, all bowed beneath the mystery aglow in the crowning aureola of the descending spring moonlight.

March 6th.

This morning we buried the American, as we have learned to call him, and as he asked, beyond the prison walls, and with the prayers of the English Church. Will his story remain untold forever, until the fullness of that time when all things are made clear—who can tell?

The name given in the criminal records is

fictitious, and his crime—a robbery from the person, accompanied by felonious assault—excludes any but the most prosaic solution.

All the members of the mess who could be spared from duty, followed the modest funeral in citizen's dress. As the first earth fell with its unnerving thud upon the coffin, a woman clad in deepest black, and so closely veiled as to be unrecognizable, stood by the grave, and said, as she threw three roses into it: "This for love, this for hate, and this for remembrance."

When the grave was filled, she walked out of the quiet cemetery, went down the white road blazing in the sunshine, where neither flowers of spring nor grasses told of the immortality of hope, and so onward into the crowded street and out of our lives forever. Out of our lives, I say, for the Sergeant de Ville, who followed, learned that her destination was Paris, the great city to the northward, which swallows yearly hundreds such as she.

Shall I ever see her again? And whom and what can such a Nemesis be pursuing? A woman of iron, this, I should say, with her heart so pecked at by the daws of fate, that she has learned to suffer and to wait, and through travail and pain to gain her end, be it good or evil, which follows.

CHAPTER II.

RUE ST. PIERRE.

UPON the morning of the 14th of April, 1879, Paris found itself, after a season of chilling rain, blessed by the brightness of a day which cheered as one of June. So sweet and gracious was this, that it gave a fictitious glamor to the grimy and shabby penitent which the city so often is in the pitiless truths of morning. The uncertain month had been cold and cheerless. Ceaseless downpours of soft rain, days of grey mist, and nights of yellow fog had made holy week appeal doubly to the frightened worldling; and Easter, haplessly, had known no star nor sun to make it the jocund day which poets sing. It was the season of daffodil and of tulip, though as yet no primroses shivered in the Bois; nor in the gardens of the Tuilleries did the early budding chestnuts bless with companionship the crocuses which wept a welcome to spring.

So, in this glorious morning the early awakening Parisians enjoyed, as a dower long withheld, the glad pipings of strange birds, the unflecked blue of the heavens, the flooding gold of the sunbeams, the soft breath of wandering country breezes, and the unvexed peace which dozed in the angles not yet invaded by the sunlight.

The quiet of early morning enfolded the city. From the Boulevard there came no lip-lipping of the tide which later floods and overflows, without ebb or lessening current, until the middle watches of the night are gone; and from the secluded and noisome districts these broad avenues surround, there rose no murmur of the labor, that, by and by, will rage impotently at the walls which bann the seas of liberty beyond.

Carriages hurrying from the Barrière Balls with the latest of their wretched dancers, flew shamefacedly up the streets; lumbering country wagons, driven by dozing rustics rumbled slowly and sullenly toward the city's walls; and when the day grew, faint as lace in the blue of the sky, the smoke from forge and factory trailed southward before the freshening breeze. Yawning shopmen opening the iron-barred doors, drew in long draughts of energy, and chatted noisily of the sad pleasures which made the sunlight of their little lives; and from Saint Antoine, workmen crawled westward, drowsy and bitter at first, but in the end loud with laughter, as the elixir of the light and breeze coursed in their sluggish veins.

As they went to their labor the Sergeant de Ville watched searchingly from the light of the broad roadway these earliest tide-rips of the flood which later overflows in labor's restless sea; and when they swept out of the Boulevard into a narrow street, which bore them to the shores of their daily tale of bricks and straw, he followed slowly, and met at its further end, coming eastward, a group of police officials.

A calm, modest street was this Rue St. Pierre, during many hours of a day which elsewhere were loud and braggart. Though not a forgotten pathway, either, wherein grasses lifted, fearfully, pale-green blades between the crevices of its paving; for it had its busy hours, and at the high noon of trade and barter, echoed with the strife of buyer and seller. But when these were gone, it rested peacefully and almost unsought, save by those who lived in the tall and gloomy houses which lined its pavement and shoved a wilderness of chimneys into the sky.

Here and there in the dingy row were a few better and newer buildings, and of these, No. 26, standing almost in the middle of the line, was perhaps the best and newest. After a moment of consultation the officials halted at this house, and then one of them pulled the bell with such a potent absolutism of authority in his summons, that, as if by magic, the door was thrown widely-open, and the concierge appeared.

Of the three officials who entered the senior was a Juge d'instruction, and the others were the Commissaire of Police of the Quarter and the Judge's clerk.

"The occupants of this house, who are they?" was the first question put to the startled woman. She enumerated these stumblingly, presented her written list and, with a shrill persistency, submitted, in proof of her truthfulness, a package of recommendations. The Commissaire carefully verified the first document, and then bowed to the Judge, who said,—

"Your list is correct. The fourth floor is occupied by a Madame Marion Darlington, an American, a widow, a traveler. So! When did you see her last?"

"An American?" replied the concierge, doubtfully. "I do not know that, as they are all English to us, except in their generosity and courtesy. But I have not seen Madame Darlington,"—and here she stopped to think and count her fingers,—"not for eleven days."

"Her apartments?"

"Have not been occupied since she left

They are locked, and by her request have been unopened; and here"—reaching to the rack—"here is the key."

"Describe her appearance."

"She was a lady, I should say; true, a poor one, but a lady, undoubtedly. Tall, thin, and not in good health; her eyes and hair were black; her face was pale and sorrowful, and usually she was very quiet—though I have heard her walking up and down, up and down, sometimes for half the night; so much, truly, that the lodger below complained; and I have heard her sobbing, often in the early morning. She spoke but a few times to us, and, so far as we knew, was without friends."

Delighted to find such patient listeners the concierge rattled away like a fusilade on a picket line, unmindful of her shabby husband, who stood in a dark corner vainly making signals of caution. Finally she said,—

"Madame Darlington arrived three months ago, and during that time no one has called upon her."

"When did you last see her,—I mean at what time of the day?" demanded the Judge.

"Upon the evening of the 3d of April she came down the stairs, slowly, as if in pain, said she was going to the country for a few days, and promised if detained beyond two weeks to write. Then she gave me, in coin, the month's advance rent for the agent."

"Describe her dress."

"Usually it was dark, though when I saw her last she wore a long cloak. I remember this, as it was the birthday of my grandson. Her sorrowful face frightened the boy, and he ran to me, crying. 'It is always so,' she said, with a sad smile, 'children never love me, and I, ah! how I could love them!' Then she called the little one and gave him a franc for his fête. As she passed out of the door, I saw that her dress was dark, and that about her she had a wrap—a cloak."

"Like this?" inquired the Commissaire; and the clerk, unfastening the bundle which he carried, showed an English cloak, soiled and stained, but not much worn.

The concierge examined this carefully, and answered, "That of Madame Darlington was new; this looks older, but the pattern is the same. I marked it closely, as I would like to have such a one for my daughter, who is poor and sometimes cold. Ah, yes! she exclaimed, looking closer, see, here are two letters,—M. D."

She pointed out the initials curiously stitched in a corner, which no one but a woman could have found. The officers looked at each other with a scarcely expressed sign of assent, and the Judge said,—

"We will now go to her apartment."

By this time the husband of the concierge had joined them, and from the partly-opened doorway of the bedroom the little grandson peered half inquiringly, half affrightedly, at the unusual scene. Climbing the stairs to the fourth story, the apartment was reached, and the door being unlocked, it was found to be an unpretentious flat of five rooms. The front faced the quiet street, the rear looked upon a mouldy court-yard, flanked by a dressmaker's workshop, wherein a dozen lazy girls were regretting the hard fortune which sent them so early to work on a day blessed by the breeze and sunshine. The sitting-room was dark and had a musty odor; its curtains were drawn and the blinds were closed, though through chinks here and there, where the wood had warped, crept rays of sunlight, which in places were broken into prismatic beams that gave color to the dancing motes.

There was but little furniture, and apparently none of those femininities which by a bit of color, or a touch of grace would have saved the surroundings from utter dreariness. Upon the walls were a few cheap lithographs, so badly hung that in their crudity and high position there was an equal fitness which bespoke a hard, untrained life. A porcelain stove standing in one corner was choked with the smooth and oily convolutions of a charred manuscript, which, though frail and crumbling, was not altogether beaten into feathery ashes. On the table lay a thick hastily sealed letter, and in the socket of a flat holder a candle had sputtered and gutted with an overflow which had filled the cracks of polished wood.

The clerk threw open the windows, and as the light and air entered, he saw in a cage upon the floor the ruffled feathers and filmy, half-closed eyes of a dead canary bird. Scattered about were the seed and sand; and on the wires the indentations of sharp teeth and a few fluffy hairs showed where a cat had tried with desperation to kill the bird. Over head was the string which had held the cage, and as the bird was taken out by the clerk, he saw that the wings were broken, as if it had beaten out its life against the wires. Surely enough, in a dingy closet off the kitchen, glared the fiery eyes of an enormous cat, fierce with hunger and wild with fear. As the clerk flung back the blinds the cat hissed angrily, and then with a bound, leaped through the casement toward a neighboring roof, tottered and fell into the dreary area.

This was all, though pitiable enough, as evidences of the sudden impulse which had abandoned to such horrors, the bird with the heavens for the marge of its freeways, and the cat, which need be a homeless wanderer nowhere. As the clerk lifted the cage, the curly-headed grandson of the concierge, who had followed them laboriously up the tiresome stairway, opened it, and stealing to his grandmother's side, sat during the examination, with the dead bird pressed against his warm soft cheek.

A thorough search showed that the gowns and linen in the armoire and chiffonière were undisturbed; and, as the concierge pointed out, that little was altered in the general appearance of the room. The manuscript upon the table was enclosed in a soiled envelope, and was addressed to Colonel Clifford Bentley, in care of the American Legation.

The officials seated themselves at the table, and after the usual formal questions had been recorded, elicited these facts:

Mrs. Darlington appeared to have no friends in Paris; she was rarely absent from home at night, took long walks by day, and read and wrote constantly. At first few letters came for her, though she appeared always to be expecting them with a nervous anxiety; finally even these failed, and every day she became paler and quieter, never ill, but evidently suffering from great mental distress. What, no one could tell, for she neither invited questioning nor assistance.

Five weeks before, on the evening of the 4th of March, the concierge brought her a letter, and early the next morning she was driven to the station for Lyons. Three days afterward she returned and since then, until the evening of the 3d, had rarely ventured out, her food being supplied from a restaurant in the nearest Boulevard.

At this point a step was heard on the stairs, and as the examiners looked inquiringly, Girard, a detective of the Main Establishment of the Sûreté entered, saluted the others courteously and drew a chair to the open window.

When the examination was concluded, the Judge said, addressing himself to the Agent, "An ordinary suicide, M. Girard, which appears to have been the result of a sudden impulse. You know the story. Eleven days since a scream was heard upon the Pont d'Austerlitz, followed almost immediately by a splash in the water and a cry for help. When Robin, the Sergeant de Ville, who was on duty at that time in the Quai de la Rapee, reached the bridge, all was quiet;

near the middle pier he found a cloak, which has been identified as belonging to the person who lived in these rooms. Yesterday evening a corpse, drifting in the tide-way past Suresnes, was brought to the Morgue; when searched nothing was discovered, by which it could be identified, except a handkerchief with the name of Marion Darlington. An inquiry showed that such a foreigner lived here, and our examination proves she has been absent eleven days. The people at the Morgue say the body has been about that period in the water; the initials of the cloak are similar to those upon the rest of her clothing; and though no identity can be established by the face of the dead woman, as, unfortunately, it is sadly disfigured, yet all evidences indicate that the drowned woman is Madame Darlington."

Girard asked and received permission to examine the rooms, and after putting a few questions to the concierge, said:

"But of the details; why, for example, should a suicide scream before the act? That, sir, seems unreasonable. Is it certain the scream was first heard?"

"So says Robin," replied the Judge.

"Robin," repeated Girard, "he who was formerly an inspector of the Sûreté?" Girard shrugged his shoulders. "Well," he continued, "Robin is not a Vidocq. But we must take this, as it is; suicide, perhaps, possibly murder—surely death—and the identity seems certain. But the motive? Pardon me, sir, but who crossed the bridge at that time?"

The Commissaire examined his notes, and read: "A young man of good height, who walked with head erect and shoulders squared like a soldier. He greeted Robin, said he had heard a cry, but that was all, and then, passing slowly toward the Place Mazas, disappeared."

"Robin did not detain him?"

"No."

"Has he been found?"

"Not yet, but we have a clue from the hackman who drove him to the Boulevard."

"The body of course," asserted the detective, "is at the Morgue?" Receiving an assenting reply, he asked the Judge, "At what hour, sir, will you summon these people for the identification?"

After the officials had consulted a moment, the Judge said the inquiry would be continued at ten.

As the clerk began to read aloud the procés verbal, Girard made his adieus; but at the landing he halted a moment, and watched a man who was mounting the stairway. When the stranger reached the floor he looked about irresolutely for a moment, and then, turning to Girard, asked, pointing to the rooms,—

"Pardon me, is this the apartment of Madame Darlington?"

Girard replied, and after the new arrival had knocked at the door, and, in obedience to the summons, entered, the detective followed. Bowing to the officials who had completed the formalities of law, the stranger said, with a foreign accent, but with an intonation which was not disagreeable to Parisian ears,—

"Gentlemen, my name is Bentley. I have been told that this room was occupied by a countrywoman of mine, an American, named Darlington,—Mrs. Marion Darlington. Is this information correct?"

The Judge motioned him to a seat and answered, "You have been correctly informed, sir. She is supposed to have committed suicide, and among the papers found is this, addressed to a Colonel Clifford Bentley."

The American took the manuscript, and after examining the address carefully, appeared to be greatly reassured, for he exclaimed in a happier tone, "This is my name, but I do not know the writer."

As he returned the document, the Judge declared: "Of course this must follow the usual forms; but I think when the legal requirements are satisfied, that there will be no delay in sending it to you in care of your Minister."

"I recognize the propriety and necessity of what you say. May I ask, has any definite conclusion been reached as to this suicide?"

"None, except that it seems to have been a sudden determination. The identification is as complete as can be expected under the circumstances."

Seals were put upon everything, and when the last formalities were settled with that definite precision which the French code demands, the party descended to the *bureau* of the concierge.

As Bentley reached the street, his calm, clearcut face brightened with a smile, and he said to the detective,—

"M. Girard, though a stranger to you, I know of you very well. There is a mystery here, and being interested, I hope to have the benefit of your advice and assistance. Will a note to the Préfecture reach you to-day?"

The Agent thought a moment and answered, "Yes, but I could not see you before this afternoon; possibly not then."

"At your convenience, I mean, of course," returned Bentley. "I live in the Rue Chaillot, and need your counsel. If you can arrange your other affairs, will you meet me to-day at five? Yes? Thanks. For the present good-bye."

As Clifford Bentley passed up the street, Girard directed the Sergeant who had been on duty at the door to follow, and, turning to the Commissaire, said, quickly,—

"Will you have Robin report to me about noon, near the Church of St. Pierre de Chaillot? You recall it—the one near the Avenue Josephine."

The Commissaire laughed quietly, and said, "Of course; but, Girard, there's nothing in this. It is a suicide without a doubt."

Girard called a fiacre, and told the driver to follow the American who, on his way westward, had almost reached the broader avenue. The Sergeant de Ville had kept him in sight, until relieved by the signal of his superior; and then, though the Boulevard widened and the wayfarers increased, the cabman never lost him; for Bentley had a striking figure, and was, as Girard had described him, "a young man of good height, who walked slowly, with head erect, and shoulders squared like a soldier."

With the keenness of a hunting dog, the driver, who knew and admired the detective, followed unfalteringly, even after the American had passed out of the quiet street and turned toward the heart of the great city, now beating madly with the fevered life of eager day.

CHAPTER III.

THE COLONEL'S STORY.

BENTLEY went directly to his apartments in the Rue Chaillot and made two memoranda of the morning's events. One of these he kept, the other he took to the Legation. Before leaving, he found the Second Secretary enjoying one of those rare moments of leisure which the hardest worked attaché in Europe so seldom has. He told his story briefly, and was promised a precis of all the information on file in the case of Mrs. Darlington.

Leaving the offices he sauntered abstractedly through the gardens to the Boulevards, until he recalled a favorite restaurant in the Rue Neuve des Petits Champs where, what time Terré was gone, they gave Thackeray the Chambertin with yellow seal. As he sat with the morning journals, awaiting his breakfast, idly watching the sunshine gleaming in the water of the carafe, and hearing, in softened echoes, the chant of the street peddlers, he turned from his newspapers to watch the bustling throng, and to drink in the life of the busy day. There was to him a compensation in this, for it drew his mind away from the misery of the past ten days and made him forget himself.

Bentley was an odd compound of active assertion and passive negation. His acceptance of most things was tempered by the hope of future struggle, his protest was ever dominated by the fear of speedy submission. With him victory often became defeat, because of his boundless pity, not only for the weak but for the conquered. He had, too, that vague unrest which is the predominant American characteristic; though in the strife of contest, as in the unvexed fields of rest, he could subordinate so perfectly this questioning of life's realities that those who knew him indifferently fancied him to be ever as calm and passionless as a Japanese idol of bronze.

He was now eight and thirty, unmarried, and not poor, though equally not rich, in the worldly sense. In figure, he was well balanced and of a good height, giving, however, the suggestion rather of physical skill than of bodily strength. His face was handsome, his eyes were black, and of a brightness which was softened by their largeness and depth; and the undisturbed calm of his features was curiously out of place with the olive complexion and the mouth of sensitive curve and play.

He had been graduated with honor from Annapolis at an unusually early age, and had done his duty thoroughly in a profession, which, of all, is the most rigorous in the demands it makes upon the physical and mental powers. During the early part of the war his service on shipboard had been brilliant, but, characteristically enough, soon after the passage of the forts below New Orleans, he resigned, entered the volunteer army, and, before the close of the Rebellion, reached the grade of colonel.

He then plunged into the whirlpool of Wall Street, and, in the days when fortunes were made and lost in the turn of a single stock, found that the life suited him capitally; not that he was a large operator, but because, with his taste for analysis, he became a sufficiently shrewd judge of the agents producing those effects which the mob accepted as causes, to have made a comfortable fortune.

But finally when speculation became a dull routine without profit, and he sold his seat in the Board, Bentley carried with him from Wall Street the kindliest regards of his associates, and left behind a reputation for keenness and coolness which became a proverb.

This was nearly two years before, and as he smoked after breakfast, he reflected, sadly enough, with what little profit the time had been passed. Presently, he strolled into the street, and after idling about, trying to arrive at a definite agreement with himself, went to the Préfecture of the Police, which was then, temporarily, in the Etat Majeur de la Garde, and left a note for Girard.

He saw by the church of St. Pierre as he entered the Rue Chaillot, a stupid moon-faced person who watched him closely, though furtively, and as he opened the door Girard appeared in the distance.

He worked steadily until nearly four o'clock, arranging papers and writing, and just as he began to doubt if Girard would come, the detective was announced.

"I congratulate you, Colonel Bentley," he said, taking the chair pointed out and beaming expansively; "you are not the man of the bridge."

"Thanks. What man of the bridge?"

"Why, our man of the bridge—the one whom Robin saw on the night of the suicide."

"Robin?" demanded Bentley. "How does he know?"

"Because he was the Sergeant who ran to the Pont d'Austerlitz, and narrowly scrutinized the only person who crossed at the time. He is certain it was not you?"

"Robin? Ah! you mean the police officer I saw at the corner where you stationed him."

Girard enjoyed this discovery and congratulated Bentley upon his astuteness.

"Oh, not at all," interrupted the American; "I saw him on the night of the third, and remembered him."

"You saw him—where?" asked the detective.

"On the Pont d'Austerlitz. He spoke to me and I answered. He was much excited, and told me that he had heard a cry and a splash, as though somebody had fallen or been pushed into the water."

"And you?" said Girard.

Bentley remained silent a moment before he added, "Yes, I heard the cry and the splash."

"But may I ask what you were doing on that side of the river at such an hour? Were you called there by business or pleasure?"

"Purely by an affair which troubled me very much," admitted Bentley. "But why this examination?"

"Because I am a police officer, and at a loss for a clue to the death of this American."

"Am I a clue? Do you connect me in any way with her suicide?"

"Frankly, yes, but to what degree I cannot say. Will you help us by revealing why you went to that quiet district and all that happened there?"

Bentley played idly with a paper-cutter he had taken from the table, and did not answer at once. Finally he said, " Well, there is not so much to tell, though I have had no rest nor ease since it all occurred. But first as to the identification at the Morgue."

"The Officier de Santé and the Juge d'instruction of the arrondisement are satisfied," returned Girard. "There were three bodies on the slabs, and the one supposed to be Madame Darlington was so battered and bruised by collisions with the piers, and boats and drift-wood that nothing positive could be asserted. The concierge and her husband were present.

"'Is it she?' demanded the magistrate.

"'I cannot tell,' cried the woman, shrinking. 'It is like her, very much like her—I think it is the lady.'

"'You cannot swear?'

"'No, but I believe this to be the person who lived in our fourth apartment—'

"'Come nearer,' growled the magistrate, you are not afraid of the dead, and in the daylight— examine closer.'

"'Spare me,' begged the woman. And then her husband came forward and said, 'My wife is right. This is the lady who lived in the Rue St. Pierre. I can swear it, and by these signs,' and he repeated, glibly enough, points of resemblance which seemed convincing."

"What is your belief, Monsieur Girard?" urged Bentley.

"So far as one person may identify another after the tides and currents and fishes have had their way, I should say the descriptions agree. In height, in figure, in costume; in the time of absence and in the handkerchief found. All these would seem to give a positive proof. Though for the handkerchief—pouf!—these people who handle the city's dead are poor and human, and, if one had an object, many things could be done."

"When may we bury her?" asked Bentley.

"To-morrow is the earliest legal limit, and after that you will be given the manuscript found in her room."

Bentley arose, went to his desk, and unlocking a drawer carefully examined a number of papers; he placed his chair so that the light fell directly upon Girard's face, and, as he watched its play, told his story; sometimes he referred to the letters besides him, and often he paused to indicate upon a map the locations of which he spoke. He began his narrative at once, and without any preface.

For many years Philip Catlin had been his nearest friend, but time, circumstances, a difference of professions and of aims finally separated them; they met, at intervals, however, until two years since, and then Catlin passed out of his life completely. Four months ago he received from Philip's sister a most pathetic letter in which, after reciting certain personal details connected with her brother, she asked that a search might be made for him through Italy and France. At her request this was carried on with as little publicity as possible, and in the end was fruitless.

Two weeks before, on the second of April, he received this letter:

"*If Colonel Clifford Bentley will be on the Pont d'Austerlitz to-morrow night at nine, he may learn something of the friend for whom he is searching.*"

Girard asked to see this message. It was signed *Marion Darlington*, and was written hurriedly and carelessly in a sharp-pointed American script.

Upon the third of April, soon after eight o'clock, Bentley drove as far as the Place de la Bastille and, leaving the cab, passed by the Arsenal into the Place Mazas. It was a dark, starless night with scarcely a ghost of a breeze, and yet filled with a rawness and a chilliness which ate to the bone. He crossed the bridge, and, after resting a moment by the last pier, strolled into the Boulevard L'Hôpital looking for the friendly assistance of a light for his cigar. Walking slowly along the street he saw, at the extremity of a blind alley that had escaped the torrent of improvement which opened the broad avenue, the red and white light of a Cabaret-borgne. Groping his way down the little street, he entered and found it to be a darksome, greasy and malodorous shop, wherein a few people, mainly of the working classes, were sitting. All were quiet and sober save a hard-looking character in blouse and cap, who was boosily apostrophising a cheap print of Gambetta which dominated the shelf whereon the bottles were ranged in death-dealing ranks. Behind the zinc-covered bar the woman of the place listened stolidly to the patriotic sentiments of the person from Belleville, and at the same time kept a wary eye,—and an evil one too, —not upon the seedy student in velvet coat and red tie and his poor, shabby Bernerette from the Quartier Latin near by—but upon the half-muffled figure of a woman who sat in a gloomy corner alone, a woman who, even in the half light, looked out of place just now in this dismal den.

Bentley, who recalled all the incidents of the

night with a memory nothing could obscure, saw that this woman kept her face hidden from view, and that in her pose there was something which told more of the lassitude of despair than of the muscular relaxation due to the cognac she had been drinking. Watching her he tried to fancy the queer fate which, at this period of life, could have brought her to a little dram-shop in the last of the *cul-de-sacs*. She might have been there earlier, it could have been the beginning of that journey when the Brasserie was a paradise of color and music; she might return there later when her sunshine was eclipsed,— but now she seemed more fit for the Café Riche, and for the life of idle bee and lavish honey, where diamonds glittered like serpent's eyes upon the shoulders she turned so coldly to the wooing of her lovers.

He had seen so many like her before, that he wondered if she was thinking with bitter regret of those happier days when she worked blithely from morn to evening, when roast chestnuts and gallete were ambrosia, and a dance at the Grand Chaumiere on Mont St. Parnasse was the offering which opened the gateway of Heaven.

Bentley called for some cognac, tossed it off with a scarcely disguised grimace, lighted his cigar, and with a salutation to the bar-woman went out of the dreary den. Even the raw air of night was a tonic after the foulness of the place, and stumbling blindly up the ill-paved alley, he heard the bell of a distant church striking the last quarter before nine.

At the Boulevard he saluted a police official and made his way quickly and expectantly to the bridge. No one awaited him. He crossed hastily, and with a growing nervousness and impatience stood in the screen of a friendly shadow until the night was noisy with the chime of clocks in spire and steeple.

"Few people had passed up to this time," he continued, in a voice strident with excitement, "and as I watched the roadway I saw finally that the bridge was deserted. Waiting until the falling mist had chilled me, I walked slowly from pier to pier, and at last, believing I had been duped, was about to go home, when I discovered a woman stealing out of the gloom from the Pays Latin side of the river.

"She moved irresolutely, but always in the shadows where through the yellow fog the lamps shone with a spectral glow. I cannot describe her even in the most general way, except that she was tall and of good proportions. She paused often as if waiting, and once she retraced her steps; but she soon turned, and with more resolution pressed forward until she reached a point nearly twenty yards from my hiding-place.

"Here a new impulse seemed suddenly to govern her, for, as if terrified, she shrank quickly behind a pier-head, and at that moment another woman rushed madly past her and onward to the centre of the bridge. Without the least hesitation this one, in a fierce desperation, climbed to the parapet, and then, with uplifted hands, and in silence, sprang into the darkness and death of the river.

"At that instant the night was smitten by a cry of terror, and as the woman I first saw reeled and fell in the pathway, there followed, above the rumble of tide and the sob of rising wind, the roar of the disturbed waters as they opened to engulf the falling body.

"Panic-stricken, I clambered to the broad shelf of stone, and as I hung over its edge, peering for some sign from the murky depths, I heard behind me the toilsome scramble of climbing feet; turning, I beheld the other woman scaling the railing beyond. When she stood upon the wide cap of the parapet, she wrung her hands in nervous terror, leaned far over, and with uplifted arms she too made ready to spring. What I called out, I cannot tell, but it held her spell-bound, and as I jumped toward her she staggered, swayed and fell—fell, thank God, —not in the angry current, but upon the roadway.

"I was dazed; unmanned, and in that moment of hesitation she gained her feet, flew shoreward, and, with a sharp turn at the Gardens, disappeared, as if the land had entombed her, even as the night and tide had drawn to death the one she had tried to follow."

Bentley shaded his eyes with one hand and with the other seemed to be exorcising from sight and memory the horrors of the night.

"What could I do?" he added. "Who would believe my story? And, besides, leaving out the probabilities of suspicion being arrayed against me, I shrank from the notoriety my unsought, innocent connection with the suicide, would bring.

"With such self-possession as I could muster, I crossed the bridge and met Robin. He was much excited by all he knew and suspected. To his inquiries, I replied that I had heard the cry and the splash, and, as he seemed helpless, I advised him to find a boat at once, and, with a bare chance of rescue, to follow the tide. Two workmen joined us, and half learning the story, hurried upon this errand, and spared me the necessity of offering an assistance which I felt would be useless. As Robin started to search the bridge, I hastened to the Place de la Bastille, and, finding my cab, was driven to the Boulevard.

"And that is all, though the horror of the scene is always with me. When I received word late last night from an official that a body answering the description given by me had been found, I went to the Morgue, and was directed to the house in the Rue St. Pierre, where I met you this morning."

Girard's experience had never been before tangent to such a circle as this. The very improbability of the confession meant much to him as proof of its truth; the confidence it implied touched him, and its general features agreed with what Robin had reported. For though Robin was a dolt from the astute Girard's point of view, he was not such a fool as the little trap laid for Bentley by the latter would have implied.

"I beg your pardon, Mr. Bentley," said Girard. "I have been doing you the injustice of believing you an ordinary criminal. You are either a very clever one or an innocent man. I think, honestly, you are the latter. But we are all apt to be rogues, you know; it is simply a question of temptation and opportunity. I am at fault, and for the present my hands are tied."

"The books," answered Bentley, in a lighter

vein, "rarely permit you this luxury. They describe you as mysterious beings, and give you the gift of discovering new worlds from the faintest shadows of the universe."

"Yes,—it reads well. That is, Monsieur Gaboriau does. No, sir; we are simply men who believe and remember trifles. Many of us have been rogues, and we catch these gentlemen, because we know how they reason. There are steps wanting in my ladder, but with patience and good luck I may find them in the end. Ah, yes! with good luck, for, after all, that is where the dramatic strokes, the *coups de théâtre* which the novelists tell of us, have their being."

Bentley's servant here brought him an official communication from the Legation. Opening it, he turned the leaves eagerly, for it was a history of the correspondence between Marion Darlington and the Minister in relation to the search for Philip Catlin. The last paragraph was a sad one. It read: "The Minister has learned from the Foreign Office that Philip Catlin, the person sought, committed suicide on the fifth of March, in the Hospital of the Convict Station at Toulon, to which prison he had been sent, under an assumed name, for robbery."

The shock to Bentley was very great, and though he felt, to some degree, guilty for his failure to find Catlin, he realized that no effort of his could have forestalled the fate which had pursued his friend.

By this time it was nearly six o'clock, and the sunlight was stealing from the sky. When Girard prepared to leave, Bentley said he would accompany him a part of the way, for this trouble urged him by an irresistible impulse to seek the scene where these tragedies had come into his life. He could not trace any explicit relation between Catlin and Mrs. Darlington, but he confessed that he owed some expiation to the poor friend who had perished so miserably.

As they rose to go the servant again entered, and gave Bentley a card. "Marsden," he read aloud, with a sudden new happiness. "So she is in Paris; thank God for that!" While waiting for the gentleman to appear, he said to Girard, "Can you remain, for we may learn something bearing on this very case."

Girard resumed his seat, just as Henry Marsden entered the room. He was a tall, well-built man, over fifty years of age, with iron-grey hair and moustache, and features that were characterized by the certain fretfulness of expression which reveals the invalid who thinks mainly of his ailments. He was distinguished in bearing, was dressed quietly in the best possible form, and his entrance and salutation fixed his social opportunities and position at once. Bentley greeted him warmly, introduced Girard simply by name, and then, after the few conventional inquiries, there intervened that half instant of constrained silence when the desire to speak in confidence is confronted by the presence of a third party. Marsden looked inquiringly at Girard, and said in French, for there was no doubting the detective's nationality,—

"I have come, Bentley, upon a matter which I desire to have considered by you, as early as your leisure will permit. It relates mainly to myself."

Bentley replied: "At any time," and, with an intuition that was the outcome of the subordination of his mental processes to the affair which had occupied and disturbed him so much of late, added, quickly,—

"May I ask you, is this in connection with a Mrs. Darlington?"

This question affected Marsden as an unexpected blow might have done. Its immediate apparent result was a nervousness that was manifested in the trembling manner with which he stroked his moustache, and turned and twisted the ring of curious pattern he wore upon the third finger of his left hand.

"Pardon my abruptness," Bentley apologized; "but this has been a season of sad surprises."

"Yes," Marsden replied, and now ignoring Girard by speaking in English, "Yes, I have come for that purpose."

"Then you may talk frankly, for we all have an interest in this woman. Monsieur Girard is an Agent of the Sûreté, and, I believe, will be of great assistance."

"We are trying to unravel this affair," said Girard, in excellent English, for he had lived at one time in the United States, "though at present we are at fault. But there are clues. Colonel Bentley, who was one, has been disappointing, in a certain sense, at least; still there are others."

"It seems, then, to be a serious affair?" Marsden asked.

"So serious," returned Bentley, "that no one can be more interested than I to find why Mrs. Darlington killed herself."

"Killed herself!" cried Marsden, rising from his chair. "Dead! She is not dead?"

Was it anguish or joy which most rang in this sudden inquiry?

When he controlled his nervousness, Marsden said: "Bentley, this makes my duty a simple one. I arrived but two hours since from the South.

I have hurried without rest from Algiers, for I hoped to have averted all chances of calamity, of disaster but, it seems now, in vain."

He took from the pocket of his overcoat several letters, and, looking at each one carefully, handed them to Bentley and explained:

"These bear directly upon the case, though they will be of little avail in proving why the mad woman who wrote them should have committed suicide. May I ask you to read them, and give me the benefit of your advice. Whatever intentions I may have had are necessarily changed by the death of this person, and I cannot act unless my way is made more clear. There are," he added, bowing to Girard, "certain objections to any one but Colonel Bentley, reading these letters; of course, should the necessity arise, we hope to avail ourselves of the experience of M. Girard—an experience which we all know to be so valuable."

At this, the detective turned towards the speaker. He had been standing at the window, apparently watching the pigeons circling above the cotes of a neighboring fancier, and listening to the interview only in that deprecatory way which would make the principals understand how subordinate his interest had now become. But, with this direct reference to himself, he brought his heels together with a snap, made his finest Continental bow, and, waving his hands in graceful curves which joined his hat and bosom, included them both in the sphere of his respectful consideration.

Marsden left the room, and, at the landing, exclaimed,—

"Bentley, this damned affair has upset me. Come and see us. We are at the old hotel, and Isabel, of course, is here."

A light of anticipation shone in Bentley's eyes, as he answered,—

"I shall give myself the pleasure of calling to-morrow; and Miss Marsden——?"

"Oh, she is very well. By the way, she said something about having met old Mrs. Harber, who has asked us to her reception this evening? Are you going?"

Bentley had not intended availing himself of his invitation, though he liked Mrs. Harber very well. The truth is, just now, he was too much hipped to join in the gayeties which the post-Lenten season had brought with disquieting frequency, but he replied, unhesitatingly,—

"Oh yes, and you may be assured I shall do my very best in this sad affair."

There was a window in Bentley's sitting-room, opening upon a narrow street, which, after deserting the main avenue, slunk into a devious route, where finally it was lost by the friendly aid of diverging by-ways. Girard was standing by this casement, and, as Bentley entered the room, had just passed a handkerchief with a quick curve before his face. From a corner where the brick walls of a garden frame this little passageway, there came an answering signal, and then Robin passing hurriedly over the open space, dove into its depths, and was engulfed in the darkness resting upon the hushed city.

Night had fallen, and as Girard made his adieus he said,—

"When shall I report again?"

"To-morrow, and thank you for coming to-day. If possible, please be here at ten."

"And you are sure," he asked, looking at the American with a glance which missed no play of feature nor any thrill of voice,—"You are sure that the other woman fell upon the bridge, and not in the river."

"As sure of it as I am that I see you now," answered Bentley.

"And she ran and was lost in the darkness?"

"She ran," repeated Bentley, gravely, "with the fleetness of a hunted deer, and was lost in the darkness."

As they stood at the landing, Bentley put his

arms upon Girard's shoulders, and turning so that the light shone clearly upon himself, said, slowly,—

"Shall I swear it?"

CHAPTER IV.

ISABEL.

FROM the beginning, the suicide he had witnessed had been a cause of profound grief to Bentley, and its mystery and the utter helplessness of his association with it made him feel that a persistent fate was darkening his days.

It was only natural that he sought constantly for any news of the drowned woman. No day passed in which he did not go to the Morgue, and there was no bridge, save one, no boat landing nor bathing float he had not visited in this sad quest. Up and down the Quais, in the broad daylight and under the starlit sky, he had walked with this grim persistency of purpose, until, at last, even the testy gentlemen seeking choice editions on the Quais Malaquais and Voltaire, knew him as well as did the gruff old soldier who sat in the sunshine and the rain near the entrance to the Pont Neuf.

But in all these wanderings he never went to the fatal bridge, for he felt that if he stood upon the spot, even for a moment, he too would climb the parapet, he too would lift his hands to the pitiless heavens, and, without a cry, he too would throw himself into the current, flowing less sluggishly perhaps, but no less certain, than the waters which have dashed in sullen fury against the arches of the Pont Royal many a mortal not half so mad as he.

The route he followed was through the Rue Bizet to the Pont de l'Alma, and so to the Pont de Constantine where, amid the throng of foot passengers, he seemed the only loiterer. But he went no further. Here for hours he would sit, always rehearsing the tragedy he had seen; and here, with straining eyes and beating heart, he would watch the moving masses on the high banks of the river, the stream creeping along with fantastic reflections of the colored boat-houses, the bridges joining their arches in its depths and the noisy boats borne upon its bosom. The life and bustle of the throngs descending the terraces were all to him a part of the great tragedy, and the murmur of the stream at night and the cool whispering of the spring-tide breezes, were a chorus of grief which the day had hushed but could not still.

When the body was found there was a sudden release to the strain upon his mind, such as might happen to a metal spring, when, under the tension of narrowing convolutions, it has reached a point of exertion, where it must break or discard the throttling force. The reaction, fortunately, was not so great as the action, though more sudden; and when he learned that between Catlin and Marion Darlington there was a relation which in some degrees justified the part he had been called upon to play, he turned hopefully, and with a livelier expectation of success, to a study of the documents before him.

After Girard left he lighted his St. Germain lamp, stirred into a friendly flame the soft coal fire which he excused as a necessity of his surroundings, and sat down to a patient reading of the papers.

In addition to the official correspondence there were four letters, three left by Marsden and one which he took from his writing desk. All of these he examined carefully, making notes for future reference, and then he put them in a large envelope, which he sealed and secreted in his desk.

The sense of exquisite relief he was experiencing shone in his face, and found an outcome in the joyousness of his mood. He hummed a jocund tune, threw back the curtains, and in the echoes of the rattling cabs, in the song of the night winds, in the subdued roar of the distant crowded streets, in the gleaming lights of the squares and parks, and in their lessening glimmer as they crept to the hill tops;—in all of these he found a lesson of hope which harmonized with the unbroken vault of lapus-lazuli sky where a crescent moon sailed upward in the glory of coming completeness.

He dressed hurriedly, and going into the street bade the driver of the cab which he had ordered to take him, by way of the Champs Elysées, to Verfours. There was a joy even in this freedom from the bondage to an idea which had hitherto impelled him when going eastward, to take the devious way by quais and bridges. His own street was quiet, for at this hour it became an unruffled corner in a current where eddies ceased to fret; but as the cab rattled into the broad avenue, he encountered the first creeping of the lesser flood, which during the late afternoon breaks full burdened at the Arc de Triomphe into estuaries that sweep placidly through the pleasant fields of fashion encircling this land of fruitful ease. As the cab drove under the opening tendrils and swinging branches of the Champs, he drew a fresher inspiration from the scene; and as the elixir of new-born content, compounded half of the night and half of his hopes, surged in his veins and warmed his heart, life seemed a better gift than he had thought it ever could be again.

After his dinner he went to a café in the Boulevard, rarely sought by the English-speaking part of his present world, and, wrapped in his overcoat, sat at one of the outside tables over a *petit verre* and a cigar. As he smoked he was joined presently by a former attaché of the American Legation, who had forsworn diplomacy for commerce, and whose lightness of character in financial affairs was excused by a perverid generosity, which showed that his perpetual pecuniary difficulties arose mainly from a foolish kind-heartedness.

"Hallo, Bentley, old boy," cried Linton, "WHERE have you been? We have missed you for an age. Have a drink? Eugene!"

Bentley did not want the cognac, though he had a fine contempt for the Phillistinism which denied it, and he did want to smoke his cigar in a quiet retrospect of the day. But he did not reject the offer, nor did he discourage Linton, who, in his own language, was "a little sprung."

"I suppose you do not care much for this tipple, though for me"—and Linton said this unaffectedly enough, but with an air which, with his costume, had made him seem foolish and foreign to his fellow-townsmen when he was last at home,—"though, for me, I am broke and can afford nothing but spirits of some sort or *vin bleu* outside the Barrière. Not that either is bad, but you are a *nouveau*, Bentley. You do not remember the old days; I do, though I was only a kid then, and my fond papa believed I was absorbing culture over here; the days when the Belleville contingent used to sing," and Linton absolutely piped up, as the reedy tenors do in the cafés chantants, with a drawl on the last syllable of each line,—

> " Pour eviter la rage
> De la femme dont je suis l'epoux
> Je trouve dans le vin a quat' sous,
> L'esperance de veuvage;
> Venez, venez, sages et fous,
> Venez, venez, boire avec nous,
> Le vin a quat' sous."

There was a tall gentleman with a hooked nose, snaky locks, a ribbon and brilliantly polished boots sitting at the next table, who manifested much silent displeasure at this canzonet; but Linton "eyed him down beautifully," as he phrased it, and so complacently, that this highly displeased person took it out of the first waiter who approached him.

"Of course, Bentley," airily continued the unabashed Linton, "my foolishness don't bother you, and do you know, if it were not for your dislike of a scene, I wouldn't mind taking a rise out of old *Ponts et Chausseés* over there, and be hanged to his sour mug, by lilting a choice bit I heard at the *Bal* last night. But I am saved the assault behold, he flies!"

The tall gentleman withdrew to a more distant table, and Linton, who was always ready for any sort of a mild row where he fancied himself aggrieved, and could forget the cause even more quickly, said, with much amusement,—

"But I say, have you heard the news? Have you seen the evening papers? No?—Eugene!" When the waiter brought all that could be found to this reckless distributor of pour-boires, Linton pointed out in each an advertisement begging a certain C. D. to return, and "all would be forgiven."

"There's a deuce of a row about this, for, as every body knows, C. D. is the charming but fiery Camille Desmoulins, who, for years, has been the evil fortune of men whose roles are star ones. Just now she has almost been the ruin of Papeéte Hoffman, as he is called, and the insensate young fool having lost her, and being afraid, it is said, of certain threats she made, has given up the detectives, and is advertising her like a patent soap."

"When did she disappear?" inquired Bentley.

"We do not know. I met Hoffman over a week ago, when he was on a terrific spree with a man named Brewer,—a countryman of ours from Denver—and he was then lamenting her desertion in bitter though alcoholic tears."

"When were these advertisements first published?" said Bentley, with as much show of interest as he could appear to take in Linton's tale.

"These endearing enticements to the obdurate C. D. have been here for three days. Curious, is it not, and all the good fishes there are in this Parisian sea. Well, it's an odd world; and, by the way, have another drink? Oh, I beg pardon! Have a drink? No gentleman ever drinks another anything. Don't smile, that is an old formula; parent, Adam; period, old red sandstone; sentence, death by hanging. You will not? Well, as we are all Germans now—*Auf Wiedersehen.*

The joyous and frivolous *flaneur* departed, saluting, and being greeted by many persons in the throng about the tables and on the pavement; and as he answered inquiries and parried thrusts with ready wit and genial courtesy the smiles which followed, showed that here, at least, the idle world, took at its best, the sunny temperament it liked so well.

As he passed slowly westward, Bentley watched him with a smiling envy, and though he knew there was no place for Linton in any world that he would create, still he could not deny his usefulness as representing Youth, Hope, Faith, Money, Paris, Paradise.

Then Bentley, for his cigar was aglow with a brightness which sent out wreathing fairy clouds wherein he saw a cheerier vista, took comfort in the thought of the work he yet might do. He dreamed of possibilities hitherto put behind as the follies of a mad ambition, and as his fancies multiplied they shaped themselves about one great hope that his lips had never dared to whisper.

He looked at his watch, and found it was time to be going; but, as he paused a moment to scan the journals, he saw in each the briefest mention of the inquiry at the Morgue, and in all the name of Marion Darlington was curiously misspelled.

When Bentley left his cab, near the Rue de Versailles, and mounted the stairs of Mrs. Harber's hotel, he confessed to an expectancy of joy which revealed how much the responsibilities he had assumed were allied with another; for apart from his sincere liking for his hostess and her amiable granddaughters he had come to this reception to meet, again and after an absence of six months, Henry Marsden's daughter.

The rooms were uncomfortably crowded, and he was a little delayed in making his bow, by a flood of visitors which overwhelmed and surprised him, as it was unusual in these somewhat exclusive seas, where the hostess believed she was not only a widowed Amphitrite, but all the other little gods and goddesses in one. When she saw Bentley, her bright, black eyes sparkled merrily, and she received him with a warmth which was effusive. He felt grateful for this marked reception, though it would have been less consoling had he known that it afforded her a much desired opportunity of keeping in petulant waiting, an unsufferable person of high official position, whose self-esteem was so out of proportion to his merits as to have the measure of a superior impertinence.

Bentley moving quietly amid the throng, found his way between the elbows and the trains with a coolness which accentuated his air of perfect familiarity with such scenes. It so happened that he knew many of the men and women about him, and, in his pilgrimage through the rooms, he emitted, to their greetings, calm phrases of salutation which cooled the air. Seemingly intent upon nothing, he was in truth, searching anxiously for Miss Marsden. At last he discovered her in a corner somewhat shut off from the ball-room by a friendly screen of foliage, where she was listening to an old gentleman, who, while talking volubly about nothing, was thinking longingly of the buffet. As Bentley went toward her, the elderly person beamed upon him as the man in the gap, and after mumbling the commonplaces with which he always covered such retreats, this ancient dandy made his way jauntily to the inner room.

Bentley saw that this departure was a mutual relief, and accepted the cordial greeting Miss Marsden gave him, not so much as a manifestation of her special gladness at the meeting, but as a votive offering for her rescue in a season of sore distress. As she stood there, framed by the greenery of the plants, Bentley thought he had never seen her looking so beautiful, and he half regretted the haste that had lost him the opportunity of studying for a while, and from a little distance, the pictures which she made.

Her figure was straight, lithe, and of true proportions; her neck rose in a graceful curve and proudly sustained a head which, by its poise alone, gave an immediate impression of her beauty; her coloring was as fresh and fair as summer roses, and her face was graced by those gifts which give to brilliancy its sweetness and to worth its innocence; for every feature told of nobility, dignity, intelligence, purity, and gentle courtesy. Her voice was soft and beautifully modulated, her intonation flowing in a rich fullness, mellowed by broad vowels and unmarred by jarring note, and of a quietness which saved it from the affectation that mistakes the faults of a social clique for the stamps of breeding. Her blue eyes looked into your own with a widespread openness, which revealed the deeps no thoughts of evil had ever dimmed; her smile gladdened as the sunshine of cool, bright mornings, and to meet her was like journeying into the heart of spring.

Without effort, and often without knowledge, she was one of those who win the honest devotion of all sorts and conditions of men, and in a confiding sincerity she gave to all an equal liking and no more. In everything which makes the sweetness and delight of womanhood, she was womanly, and others, jealous of her success, who could not deny this charm, confessed in moments of self-abasement that, after all, the crown of woman is womanhood. To-night, as Bentley always remembered, she was dressed in white, which was relieved by a corsage of sun-flecked Maréchal Niels; and spanning the soft lace which wreathed her bosom, as silver mists at sunset sleep on tinted clouds, she wore an open-work Spanish brooch, which displayed in quaint and picturesque lettering, the word YSABEL.

"I heard of your arrival only to-day," said Bentley, "and I need not say how glad we are, for you have brought the spring, and the thanks of *tout-Paris* should be a compensation for this exile from the South."

This was unusual, even such a commonplace little compliment, in Bentley, and, smiling brightly, she answered,—

"Oh, no! I do not regret the South; we are birds of passage, you know."

In a few moments they were in the full tide of reminiscent talk; this, on Bentley's part, to hide the joy the meeting brought him, and on hers, to hold the happy mood which revealed his character in a newer light.

Their acquaintance was not an old one; for though Bentley had known Marsden for many years, it was only in the last summer he had met Isabel. He had been idling away his days in Holland, and, for pure lack of intention in any other direction, had gone to Denmark. Here, at Marsden's request, he went with them on a six weeks' trip to the North Cape; later, there had been a chance meeting in the Engadine, and then they separated, leaving him with a sense of loneliness which was a new factor in his life.

"It is a pleasant place," he said, "this Europe; and I half regret to go away, even for a little while,—one can be so lazy here without reproach or effort,—but in a few weeks I may have to leave for India."

"And we are on our way home," she replied.

Bentley had not known this, and, with a disappointment which he did not try to conceal, he answered,—

"I am sorry to hear that, as I had hoped to meet you next summer in England. At the worst mine is but a flying trip, and I confess it will be a regret not to find you here upon my return." The sadness of the separation depressed him, for he asked, despondently, "Are you glad to go home?"

She replied with earnestness, "Naturally, for I have longed these many months for the freer air and wider commons of America. To me there is no place like it, though, of course, I quite understand in many ways what foreigners say of it and of us. But, indeed, I am so glad to return, that I hope never to come abroad again."

"You have been in Rome?" he inquired, lending himself to her enthusiasm.

"Yes, this winter; and for the first time I did not drink of the Fountain of Trevi."

Though Bentley smiled at the quickness which had solved his question, he was touched by the *mal du pays* trembling on her lips, and by the tears which glistened in her eyes, as diamonds in the depths of encircling sapphires. He knew she was abandoning of her own will, and gladly, social opportunities which mean much to women, and turning to another vein, he said: "Then you are safe, and, if it is a comfort to hear this, let me tell you we will miss you; not," he added, thoughtfully, "because there are so few here,—I mean among the exiles,—who have even a sentimental fancy for home, but because life will be different for many who cannot follow."

Marsden joined them at this moment, and with some excitement began airing his opinions of the American colony; Bentley laughed quietly at the tremendous condemnation the harangue seemed to imply, and said, as he was about to go: "Well, this house in any event I like, and, as I must say good-bye, you may be sure I, at least, will be as sincere as its hospitality deserves."

As he came from the room where he had left his overcoat, Marsden stopped him.

"We are going also, Bentley. By the way, have you read the letters?"

"Yes, carefully."

"What do you think of them?"

"I think," Bentley replied, not caring to give a more definite answer, "the woman was demented, and that you have acted with discretion."

"You have said nothing to my daughter, in any way, of this affair?" inquired Marsden.

"Nothing; but can you come to my rooms to-morrow?"

"To-morrow? yes, with pleasure."

"Shall we say at four?"

Marsden thought a moment and answered: "I regret not—but can you make it five o'clock? Yes? Well, expect me, without fail."

Bentley turned to go, and Marsden, whose manner was certainly very good when he cared to make the effort, hesitated, and then exclaimed, with a pleading which he could not control,—

"Bentley, I feel this affair terribly, mainly now, as it seems to be without remedy. I fear it for my daughter's sake, because I realize what this suicide would mean, should she ever hear of it. Help us out of it, will you not?"

As Clifford Bentley slowly walked down the street in the cool starlight, he saw, framed in a carriage window and making sunshine in his night, the sweet face of Isabel Marsden, and he knew he would serve her to the end.

CHAPTER V.

A QUEER LOT.

WHEN Girard came the next morning, Bentley learned that all arrangements had been made with the arrondisement agent of the Pompes Funébres for burying Mrs. Darlington in Montmartre. The detective had nothing new to report, and seemed to be disturbed by the inscrutability of several mysteries which, of late, were reflecting unfavorably upon the reputation of his corps.

Bentley asked the police theory of the advertisements which implored C. D. to return, and found that Camille Desmoulins, the subject of the inquiry, was, as Linton had said, a *demi-mondaine*, whose history was written in short paragraphs, and punctuated with exclamation points. Girard knew the salient points of her record thoroughly.

She was a child of the dregs, born, heaven only knew where, and brought up, heaven only could tell why, by Mére Blinder, the chiffonière. After being graduated from the gutters of the Rue de la Chapelle, she was sold for an obolus to a young thief, who starved and beat her, until one day she betrayed to the police his share in a crime which sent him to Cayenne for life.

She then lived as these Pariahs exist everywhere, and finally, at a Barrière Ball, danced herself into the affections of a tradesman who gave her a decent training, lavished the profit and capital of his shop upon her, and when she deserted him for a Bohemian journalist, killed himself outside her door. Girard remembered her perfectly, and told, with an unctuous appreciation of successful villainy, how she had risen on her ladder, step by step, till at last a day came when she played no inconsiderable part in the drama of that lesser society which sometimes rules the greater.

She was, the Agent said, the worst woman he had ever known—one of those veritable daughters of the devil who, with the demureness of a *rosière*, and the face of a saint, ruin more families than the worst of fraudulent bankers. The golden days of her triumphs were amid the sympathetic surroundings of the empire's dissolution, but of late her star had waned.

For over a year she had held in the meshes of her deviltries young Hoffman, the son of a merchant, who had left an enormous fortune, made by a trade monopoly with the Marquesas and Tahiti. The *ménage* had not been an unhappy one, until this quarrel, which, though not the first, by any means, was, Girard believed, their last. What had brought it about, no one knew, but it must have been most serious, for, as Camille left the house, she swore by one of the oaths which these women keep for a final restraint and seldom violate, that she would never see him nor his world again.

Hoffman had heard these threats before, but only when they were shrieked or sobbed in the idleness of an anger which expected consolation, and, for a time, he did not worry over her disappearance. He was a fat, blonde Alsatian, with merry blue eyes, the face of a dissipated cherub, and the heart of a fairy godmother; indeed, he was much too good a fellow to sow his wild oats for such a reaping, and, in the end, proved to be a regenerate and shining mark. He had a sincere liking for Camille, though a little wearied by her temper; and she, so her rivals confessed with pity, really cared more for him than for the others—the dozens—she had blown from her fingers.

He sulked for a week, gambled beyond any sort of prudence, and lost a considerable sum at baccarat to that mysterious Captain Marker Blunt, late (so his cards said) of H. B. M.'s Fourteenth West India Regiment, whose good luck was as unquestionable as his skill in hitting the bull's eye at any number of paces with any weapon. When Hoffman felt satisfied that both cards and love were equally unlucky, he settled down to a premeditated dissipation, which was cheerless; he drank potions fathoms deep —not only straight and mixed, but interspersed with reviving cocktails, compounded by a gifted acquaintance from Denver, named Brewer.

Of course, this upset his weak and good-natured head, until, finally, he reached a stage where delirium tremens awaited complacently the next bout. As usual, Brewer was unimpaired—for his capacity was large, and the discretion which confined him to one tipple, great; so, while Hoffman was dimly seeing the preparatory angle worms, which would develop into the conventional snakes, Brewer was as fresh as the breezes fanning his native mountain-tops, and as thirsty as the alkali plains lapping their foothills.

But Brewer had, as he boasted, "sand and sense," so, corralling Hoffman, he dragged him to the Russian Baths, and had him steamed, rubbed, kneaded, scrubbed, and generally inundated into a state of comparative sobriety. He took his patient home, bribed the servant with a napoleon to swear there was no more liquor in the world, and left him to a sleep soothed by bromide, and blessed with the expectancy of awakening to a "*Sure cure for Jim-jams in the earlier stages*"—the prescription for which Brewer had received from a friend, whose experience in these matters—personal and ancillary—was the most profound in Colorado.

With sobriety came the remembrances of his lost Camille, and Hoffman rushed by the first and fastest train to Normandy. He had often listened to the pathetic story of her early life. The happy village, the companions of her childhood, the green—blithe with song and dance; Basil, the inn-keeper, and Jacques, his son; the conscription, vows and tears; and the parting salute of the soldier as he stood in the sunset on the hill and waved his last good-bye. Then the tempter from the wood-embowered chateau on the mountain; the ghost-haunted woodland walks; the little gift; the gathering of wondering peasants at Basils, and the short dispatch which told how Jacques had died at Gravelotte, with his face to the foe and a prayer for her. More tears and more despair, followed by vows of love which could never die; the stern papa looking down from the centuries of family portraits, and the haughty mamma sheathed in satin, which rang as the winds from the seas in the forests of Barbesac. The flight; the deserted inglenook; the search; the moaning mamma, and Paris. Desertion; the heart aweary of life, hungry for death; then Paradise, Hope, and Hoffman. She told it all, as Watteau sketched, as Van Loo painted, as Crébillon the Gay dreamed.

Our weeping Alsatian found the village of Barbesac, and nobody who had ever heard of Camille, except that, five years ago, she had been at its castle with a gay party, whose eccentricities had become a legend of Black Magic in that peaceful land. Hoffman returned to Paris, disconsolate, but not disenchanted, and put the affair into the hands of a bureau of private detectives.

"But these apprentices," Girard growled, with professional jealousy, "these dolts so mismanaged their trust, that last evening M. Hoffman was compelled to seek the regular police."

The advertisements were immediately discontinued, and through systematic search the woman was traced from her pretty house in the Champs, to a dingy cabaret in the dreariest *cul-de-sac* of the Quartier Latin; and there she disappeared as if the earth had swallowed her, "and by to-morrow," groaned Girard, "those blockheads of the private Bureaus, who are nearly as bad as our imbeciles of the *Police des Moeurs*, will be sticking their tongues in their cheeks at us."

"When did this woman leave Hoffman?" asked Bentley.

"About six o'clock on the evening of the third."

"You say she went to a wine-shop south of the river; was this the *Cabaret Duplan*, at the end of a mean little street, not far from the Boulevard l'Hôpital?"

"I am not regularly on this duty, but let me read the facts," responded Girard, with a sudden alacrity, as he took out a shabby note-book, which entombed the skeletons of more tragedies than all the poets from Euripides to Shakespeare have sung.

"*Mais oui*—yes; the *Cabaret Duplan*, that is right. Ah!" he said, for Bentley in the narrative, had told him nothing of this part of his story;—"and so, M. le Colonel, you were the foreigner of whom we could find no trace. You left there soon after eight; you recall, perhaps, that you spoke to a Sergeant de Ville, and then turned toward the river. True—it is all plain—this was the night of your adventure on the bridge; when you left him, the police officer walked down the street, saw this woman in the cabaret, and twenty moments later was called from his station to stop a row in the Brasserie *Au Petit Gamin*. When he returned to his post, the woman had gone, and with her all our clues."

"I spoke to the Sergeant, as you said, and it must have been at the very time he was at the Brasserie, that the woman—the two women—came over the bridge."

"Could Camille Desmoulins have been one of these, and if so, which?" wondered Girard, —"Well, it is a clue, and I thank you in the name of the Agency. But with your permission, I will ask one more question,—Was the woman drinking when you saw her? Yes? Ah! that was her habit at times, and it made her crazy. She poisoned a man once, we all believe, though we could not prove the crime. She was mad for a week, and they feared it would be the insane asylum in the end. Alive or dead, let me tell you this, Colonel Bentley, she was and is a devil. She was a monster, none so bad in my experience, and with the face of an angel; and those always are the most terrible."

Soon after noon a simple funeral crawled the steep streets of Montmartre, and under the bright sunshine of an unflecked sky Marion Darlington was buried. When it was all over—and he waited until the very last—Bentley walked sadly out of the cemetery, and went, aimlessly, for a long stroll to the hills and plains where the defences of the city lay.

He returned at four o'clock and found that the

Minister of Foreign Affairs had forwarded him, through the Legation, the manuscript left by Mrs. Darlington. At five o'clock Marsden appeared, and after the first courtesies had passed, Bentley said, pointing to the dead woman's letter,—

"The story is now complete; if you are ready, we will go over this sad business together."

The perpetual impression of pain and discomfort which Marsden gave was intensified to-day. He always saw fit to go out in search of misery, and just now, was toying with a particularly sombre Amaryllis, who was moaning in the shade of a vault. In his present mood he would have started in fairly, and relieved his mind by saying something disagreeably personal; but, fortunately, he had a wholesome respect for Bentley, and resisted the craving. He felt that this friend read him thoroughly, for with all his pretence Marsden was shallow; he was narrowed to a stock of phrases, which were as clear cut—and deep—as intaglios, but as these seemed rare to the common and passed for objects of curiosity, he had obtained a fictitious reputation for cleverness. That Bentley measured him accurately, he was certain, and therefore his choice stings were saved for others who took him at his own valuation.

He fumbled with the letters, shuffled his chair

into the best light, and in an aggressive, irritable way told of his first relations with Mrs. Darlington. They all came through Philip Catlin. "This fellow," he began, thumping the table with his wrinkled forefinger, "who has made the trouble, was, to my mind, a confounded cad. Yes, I know, Bentley, he was your friend, and is dead, and we ought to govern our feelings by a respect for cheap mortuary philosophy, and all that, but I must be honest, and,—well, let us compromise and say—Catlin was a poor lot. We met him first at Saint Augustine, some time early in—let me see," he counted his fingers, "'79, '78, '77. Yes, some time about the New Year of 1877.

"I had a half acquaintance with him, and knew vaguely that he had been badly caught in the Street during the whirlwind of '73. However, here he was in Florida instead of trying to earn a respectable living, in perfect health, and yet moving about in a feeble, shiftless idleness that set my teeth on edge. And then, confound it, he was forever in the way,—that is, in my way,—so much so, that he took all the comfort out of existence. He would hang around for hours, doing nothing but dreaming, always agreeing with me as he did with every other shade of opinion, and always in a feeble-minded way, which gave him the reputation of being 'so gentlemanly.'

"How do you suppose, my good friend Bentley, how do you suppose it ended? He wanted to marry my daughter! Fell in love with her, as he was pleased to call it. I know you think I am telling this in a coarse way, but it is the truth. He was man enough to see me first, and to take my emphatic refusal in a style that was not undignified. The next day, to my infinite relief, he went away, after announcing publicly that he was going up the Ocklawaha on a second trip. Fancy anybody who is, presumably, low in his mind, making a second time that awful trip, and in February, when Florida is black with the hordes of wild Western tourists.

"My daughter took his departure quite as a matter of course, for she never suspected his feelings, and I was delighted to see that she played tennis in the Fort and went out in the cat-boats with as much zest as ever. This did me a world of good, for the truth is, Catlin had become a tremendous nuisance."

Bentley listened with increasing annoyance, for Marsden was telling a sad story brutally, and was hard with the dead man for no other reason than that he had ventured to love Isabel in a manly straightforward way. He began to believe this battered old broker was without a heart, and that he valued more how things looked, than what they meant, where they lead, or what useful end to humanity their accomplishment might serve.

But in this he misjudged Marsden. It is true that this dissatisfied, selfish creature would have said his prayers by proxy and thought himself quits with Heaven for any benefit received, but Isabel was his world, and in an irritable, though a perfectly loyal way, he endeavored by unselfish care to make amends for his neglect of her dead mother.

In June of the same year the Marsdens sailed for Europe. As nothing in the meantime had been heard of Catlin, the irascible father's anger and surprise were not without some reason when, one afternoon, in the Champs Elysées, he beheld the gentleman standing lazily within the barrier rope of a mountebank, and watching with uproarious joy the woes of Polichinelle.

Catlin did not see them often at this season, though he was zealous in the endeavor; but when they returned to Paris in October, he was soon mooning around Isabel in the old fashion, while, ostensibly, very busy collecting evidence for the French Spoliation Claimants.

Marsden's treatment, even from his own account, must have been a delightful study in blizzards, and Catlin's cheerful acceptance developed a latent torridity of temperament that was phenomenal.

In January the Marsdens went to Nice, and later to Pau, where they passed a delightful winter, and when, in the spring, they returned to Paris, Catlin was still there, though it was obvious he was having a severe struggle with the Claims, and was more or less down at heels, materially and physically. Marsden met him by chance one day, and gave him a fishy hand in return for the effusive warmth with which Catlin greeted him. He asked delightedly after Miss Marsden, and, without the slightest preface or pretence, said, as they separated,—

"You see I am not changed in the least, Mr. Marsden; I shall never change, and if persistency will do it, I shall succeed in the end."

"Somebody told me Catlin had been drinking more than was good for him," continued Marsden; "but I do not believe this was true. I noticed a certain unsteadiness, a want of method, a wildness,—as if he were being pursued by a terrible fate he could not escape,—but no signs of dissipation. Though he did not go about much, some old friends of his mother asked him at times to their parties, and we occasionally saw him.

"After returning from our rambles last summer,

we met him again. His manner had entirely changed, and there was no longer a question that he was in sore straits; it was evident, too, he had taken to dissipation in some form.

"I pitied him,—'pon my soul I did, Bentley,—and when, after putting myself to considerable inconvenience by interfering in an affair which did not affect me, I offered to make definite arrangements for his return home, he ungratefully and most impertinently said,—

"'Thank you, no. I am here for a purpose which you understand; and it is, after all, simply a question between my devotion and your obstinacy,—I mean your objections. I am satisfied that when your daughter learns how truly and unselfishly, in the midst of horrible sufferings and self-denials you cannot measure, I have cared for her, she will pity me; this, by association, I hope, —and I am willing to take my chances,—will ripen into a stronger feeling.'

"I could have kicked him for his cool impudence, but, Bentley, there was something in his manner which made me respect him then more than ever before.

"I never saw him again. In January we went to Nice, and the day after my arrival I received this letter, which had followed me for two months."

He took up the letter marked No. 1, and read it slowly,—

"126 Baltimore St., Philadelphia, Penn.
"November 2d, 1878.

"DEAR SIR:—The unaccountable disappearance of Philip Catlin has awakened so much serious anxiety that I am induced to ask you, as being in the best position to know, if you will send the latest news in your possession to the above address, and oblige, "Very sincerely yours,
"MARION DARLINGTON."

This was in the same handwriting as the note received by Bentley on the second of April.

"I answered this," resumed Marsden, "and, as I thought under the circumstances, with great civility. We had not seen Catlin since October, and I put this as clearly as I knew how, but with so little success, that three weeks afterward I was forwarded, by my bankers in Paris, the letter, which is marked No. 2,—

"PARIS, January 28th, 1879.

"SIR:—Philip Catlin is currently reported to be betrothed to your daughter; some say, they are secretly married. I do not believe either report, for he is incapable of an act so dastardly, of a want of faith so dishonorable to us both. But I have also learned that if there be the slightest truth in these charges, the reasons for the secrecy lie with you.

"I have endeavored to find him everywhere, but in vain. He is poor and powerless. To disappear, save by death, one must be neither; and I can not resist the belief that you are primarily accountable for his absence, and this in your daughter's behalf.

"You have money, friends and influence; I am poor, alone and powerless. You must find him or take the consequences, for the burden of my sorrow is too great to bear without hope. You can give me peace; I can bring you trouble. If I were not desperate I would prefer the former; as it is, I am careless as to the issue.

"You may, in a calm philosophy of bloodless scorn, call me melodramatic and turn me over to the police. But you dare not, and, I warn you, not as a threat, but as a light to guide you, that I have sworn Philip Catlin's fate shall be your daughter's."

"I know that this is hardly the way to approach a man of the world, nor would I do so save for my sore trouble and for the knowledge that behind the machine lies the father. I have not reached your pity, but I can and shall, through her, reach your fear. Not only by her present ignorance, but by the faintly remembered griefs of her childhood, when you killed, as surely as man ever murdered, your wife and her mother, not by blows, but by sugar-coated horrors.

"It is your association with that mother, who is a dream to her, which sanctifies you; it is your necessity for that association which arms me."

"Shall it be peace or war? I am not stalking as a tragedy queen, nor do I ask a favor. I am a wronged woman, and it is my right, as the affianced wife of Philip Catlin, to demand this relief."

"Henry Marsden, Esq., "Marion Darlington,
 "Rue Scribe,   "26 Rue St. Pierre,
  "Paris."   "near the Boulevard Beaumarchais.

Although Bentley knew these letters by heart, he thought it best Marsden should tell the story in his own way. But at this point he doubted the wisdom of his judgment, for the spell of the mad creature's threats, now so impotent and averted, still enchained Marsden with a power which displayed itself in an emotion that overmastered him.

Then, too, he realized he had done Marsden a wrong, and that this mass of concentrated selfishness loved his daughter with an intensity which was undoubted, even though its strength was drawn from the expiation owed to his past. In those days of recklessness it had been a pet aphorism of Marsden that the land of marriage was one which foreigners would invade and natives fain escape; and in the practices which he essayed he tried to still the self-reproaches for his escapes by the successes of his invasions. So when after years of a devotion which was as beautiful as it was unrequited, his martyred wife died, Marsden learned with a sudden affright and an awful regret how much this uncomplaining woman had been in his life.

In the spring time, after the first wooing was over, he had idly pursued the selfish desires of his days so long, that the summer died untimely, and there was for him no leaf, nor grass, nor sheaf; and when the fruitless autumn faded in the winter's snow, he turned, in his season of despair, with a wild repentance to the girl who had been the heaven of the mother lying dead.

Happy for him was it when love, in the anguish of neglected opportunities, dreamed of a second harvest,—happy, indeed, that such a flower of beauty and of truth awaited, and not the stubble and the wasted grain, and the barren fields, which never would bloom as of old.

Let it be said that the prayers he made in those afterdays for both were holy ones, and that the promises he offered in expiation were kept—with a hard, unyielding affection, if you please, and with selfishness—but still with a love, which, in a blind way, impelled him to do his duty by his child.

It was true, also, that Catlin's poverty had not counted against him, for, as Marsden had sworn that death alone should separate father and daughter, he used fondly to say that a poor man was surer held than one who was rich. But, apart from the fact that he did not want his daughter to marry, Catlin's weakness excited a personal antagonism which he could not overcome; and he feared, in trying to gain his point, that Catlin, who knew the story of his second marriage, might not scruple to disillusion Isabel. He did not stop to consider the folly of any such belief: he simply accepted it as a possibility, and let it rule him.

"I confess, Bentley," he resumed, when the strength of his emotion had subsided,—"I was afraid of this devil, mainly for my daughter's sake. You know our world, our *metier*, our opportunities, our ideals, our temptations. In the past, I was as other men, who are deficient on the side of sentiment, and I acted thoughtlessly—perhaps, worse—to the sweetest and most forgiving woman who ever lived. But," he explained, as if trying to justify his sins by impeaching the race, and specially including Bentley, "we look upon these things so differently from women."

It was evident he was groping for words wherewith to soften his confession; but these did not come easily and proved that it was only the necessity of making his actions plain which could have moved him to disclose his weaknesses, even to a person whom he respected and liked as much as he did Bentley.

"In short, I feel now I might have done differently; not that I have been a rogue or a scoundrel, but, in my life, there have been events, which, if revealed to my daughter as simple, statistical moral facts, without the color, the light, the apology of the circumstances which dominated, and gave them a *raison d'etre*,—why, I fear she would hate and leave me for the first adventurer, who posed as an elementally proper person, possessing the merits I never could have known.

"I sent Miss Darlington a note, which, as I hoped, smilingly put the question by; but she never answered it. This alarmed me, and I seized upon the pretext of my illness to write another in which I blustered a little, and rapped up a fictitious policeman. Her only reply to this was a telegram, which read—'*Find Philip Catlin for me.*'

"Her determination seemed so fixed that I employed an Agent of the Sûreté, who brought the best recommendations from the Central Bureau. On the fifth of March, I came into possession of the letter which is marked No. 3. It was addressed to my daughter, and was sent by a messenger, whom, fortunately, the detective intercepted at the office of the hotel. The address on the envelope was so cramped and unnatural, that the more I studied, the better I became satisfied it was in a disguised hand. I kept it two days, and, after weighing all the arguments, felt it was my duty to open it. Thank God, I did! for, as I had suspected, it was written by that fiend."

This letter, unlike the others, was put aside by Marsden, though it was needed to complete the missing links of the story, and ran as follows:

"Toulon, France.
"March 5, 1879.

"I have come from the death-bed of the man you have murdered; to-morrow I shall see him buried where only strangers sleep. Philip Catlin—the truest, bravest, and brightest soul in the world—died by your hands, a felon in the Toulon jail. It is true, he killed himself, but this was in remorse for his desertion of me, and because the degradation to which you sent him could be endured no longer. As he died, I shall try to make you die; not to-day, perhaps, nor to-morrow, but some day,—and, if it can be—amid horrors more dreadful than those which surrounded him.

"As you tried to win his love from me, I shall take from you—in my own way and time—the love that is most to you. I send you this prophecy from the dead past of my ruined life. I consecrate my oath by the touch of the flowers I shall throw in his nameless grave to-morrow.

"With every prayer I make for him, I ask an evil for you, and with the shadow of his death still clinging to my lips, I dedicate your days to the anguish mine have known; I pray every moment of them may be cursed with grief, and hunger, and pain. I pray that the death, which you fear, will be about you, ready to strike in the moment when it will be most awful, and, that the death you beg for, will wait and wait—before it comes—until you know, as I have known, the maddening terrors of hell.

"Marion Darlington."

"That night," Marsden continued, "I went to Marseilles, and, by the tenth, I was in Algiers, living in a quiet villa, near the gardens of the Bab el Oued. But I could find no rest. Whether Catlin was dead or not, this woman was insane, and I knew not at what moment she might wreak the vengeance she had invoked. At last, in an agony of terror, I determined to come here, to consult you, to undergo any sacrifices which would placate her. Her death made all this useless, though there are revenges which are as sure to the dead as to the living, and, in some mad way —yet to be revealed—she may have left a legacy of hate to finish the misery she began in life."

When Marsden brought his narrative to an end, Bentley broke the seal of the manuscript found in Mrs. Darlington's room, and said,—

"Since your share, sir, in the mystery of this woman's life and death is greater than mine, I have kept her last message until you came. Are you ready to hear it?"

Marsden made a gesture of assent, and Bentley read slowly as follows:

"TO COLONEL CLIFFORD BENTLEY.

"*Paris, April 3d, 1879.*

"This night I go to my death,—for all I love, even my revenge, so far as it would make me live, is dead. I have struggled for a month in vain. Morning and evening, day and night, I have heard a voice whispering—'Come, now is the time—leave behind all this—come;' and I can no longer resist its pleading. I make you the heir of my wrongs, and I am driven to kill myself, because of the woman whose life is mixed with his, with yours, with mine,—even to the end and for their evil. She is Fate. Catlin could not escape her, nor I—can you? She is beautiful, but it is the beauty of the devil which is given to kill, not the body alone, but the soul. She has killed mine, she has killed the man who loved you so dearly—she will kill you.

"Philip Catlin was my affianced husband—the only human being in all this world who ever gave me a loving word or touched my hand in tenderness; for since my earliest years I have been an orphan, without a memory even of the mother who might have straightened my warped life, of the father who is said to have left us both to die unheeded. But I needed nothing, hungry as I was for human sympathy and love, after Philip came into my life. It was a brief dream, and she awakened me.

"He followed her to Europe, as one demented, and to be near her, struggled and starved. She was the lure light, he the foolish moth. But hers was the light of a wicked spell, and his the trial through which all true love must go, for he loved me best, and only me. When this woman left Paris, she cheered him with promises of her return,—and to be near her he lived in the most abject poverty and underwent sacrifices which broke him down in mind and body.

"Then you met her, and it was Philip's bitter grief to learn that his best loved and oldest friend was the rival who complicated the struggle. Can you imagine the strength of my love when I tell you that I, who had risked and lost all, would have welcomed gladly their marriage to have saved him. For he would have tired of her, and, if not, I could, at least, have killed her. But no; with a refinement of cruelty called pity, she would neither let him go nor stay, and in a moment of madness, he determined to follow her to the South.

"He was more fit for the Hospital and the tender care of those who loved him than for such a journey. Before he reached Lyons, he was robbed while asleep in the crowded car, and awoke to find himself at the station alone and penniless. For two days, up and down, up and down, through the streets of that prosperous city, he walked, seeking the thief, and starving.

"He had ten sous left.

"Five of these he gave to a beggar who beseeched alms in the name of God's mother, and following this cripple he saw the money spent, in the nearest shop, for brandy. He struggled and starved another day, sleeping in the rain and mire, and always hearing a voice which opened a way for escape. He went to the agents of the large American silk houses, and told his story,—in one case to a countryman,—but all spurned him, he who had been a soldier, and was a gentleman.

"He spent two of his five sous, not for bread, as that hunger was gone, but for brandy; and the fierceness of desire growing upon him, the rest of his pennies followed. Then he became demented—as irresponsible as the child, as the madman whom all excuse. He heard the voice still calling—it seemed always the same: 'Come to me,' it sang, 'and elysium.' How do I know these things? He wrote them to me in the letter which I burned. You will find its ashes, choking the stove in my room, when I am dead.

"After this came madness.

"The police charge him with having violently seized at noon, in broad sunlight, and on the most crowded street of Lyons, a bank messenger who was carrying money to be deposited. Philip, in his delirium, asked the man to deliver one of the bags peacefully as a loan which would enable him to reach Nice—to follow her. Instead of pitying him, as one would a child reaching for the moon, the brute struck him. A struggle followed, such a short, such an easy one,—and it was called heroic by these miserable Frenchmen. They arrested, tried and convicted Philip, surely and speedily, for he made no defence, and these things are ordered by a machinery which in France never fails for foreigners.

"When in the cool, quiet jail, under the pitying hands of the Sisters, he came back to life, he accepted his fate without a protest. His sentence was imprisonment at hard labor for ten years, at home, as they tried to call it, and not in Cayenne. While we were searching, and when Marsden's stolen money could have found and saved him, he was praying for death amid the nameless, relentless cruelties of a common jail. He failed day by day, almost hour by hour, they told me, from the very beginning, though they were as good—the naval surgeons—as the civil rules allowed.

"Finally he died.

"Just before the end, his reason returned, and he thought of me, and wrote what I am entering here for you, our avenger. He told me all, how he had been spurned like a rabid dog by the father, and how he felt that he must make one last effort or die. He asked my pardon for the past, my pity for the present, my prayers for the future, for his misery could be endured no longer, and he had the means—a common enough poison—of killing himself.

"It was his last good-bye to the world, and of all created things to whom did he send it—to her? No! To me? Yes! for he loved me. It was my first clue, and though I did not dare telegraph the authorities, lest a punishment might be inflicted upon Philip, I determined to save him.

"I went to Toulon at once, and having gained admission to the prison, reached him, my Philip, reached him in time—to rescue, to ease a single pain? No—to see him die!

"And this was all, all after the years of patient love and waiting.

"At first I determined to bide my chance and kill her who had brought these evil days upon us, but that desire is gone now, and you, not I, must be the agent of the vengeful Fate in whom I believe. I leave her to a worse death than I can give, to your contempt, to your knowledge of what she is.

"I know she will die as he did, and if spirits can return, I shall be with her. And you, will you love a murderer? Will you deny that behind the mask of the angel is the face of the devil? Will you be led as he was, differently in way, but no less surely, to the same end?

"The night is coming, and my last message on

earth is for you. I leave it in this room which has known my grief, lest my strength should fail on the bridge, where I shall seal the truth of what I try to tell you, with my life. If you are not there, take these as the last words of a woman who will be dead when you read them. Do not pity me,—I am beyond the need of that,—but be warned by
"MARION DARLINGTON."

Bentley read steadily to the end, and when he looked up, saw that Marsden was watching him intently.

"Do you believe her?"

"I pity her. She was insane! But what untold evil she could have wrought. Thank God, I never met her."

"But, do you believe her?" insisted Marsden.

"I believe she loved Catlin with a strength which turned her brain after he rejected her. Hers was a sad life, I fancy, with it all,—and I doubt if she ever had the even start that we, and most of us, were given. I blame and pity her."

"What will you do with these papers?" asked Marsden, who avoided the subject when it reached a stage of defence. "Surely no one else should read them."

"Only one other—Catlin's sister. Her right is the greatest of all," exclaimed Bentley.

Marsden walked up and down the room, went to the window, nervously lighted a cigar, smoked fiercely for a moment, as if trying to quiet his emotion or to arrive at a decision; and, not looking at Bentley, finally said,—

"Tell me, is this dead woman as insane, in speaking of the revenge she leaves to you, as she is in all other things?"

"Do you mean by that—do you intend to ask —if I love your daughter?" answered Bentley, quietly. "Yes, thank God, that knowledge of higher things is mine, however vain my love may be. Let me tell you. Not to you is it so great a surprise to learn this, as it would be to your daughter. You will say,—pardon me," he added, with a courteous gesture, as Marsden was about to interrupt,— "you will say, and justly, that I have seen so little of her. But it is not always that, and I only know my feelings are as I have told you."

It was a profanation for Bentley to reveal this secret of his life, even to Marsden; but he could not escape the duty it had become. "She, of course," he continued, "will never suspect nor know it from me; for I realize too well the uselessness and unfitness of my life and character, to harm her even by the thought that I could aspire to the heights whereon she lives. I know my own unworthiness in every way. But this I can do. Some day you may think she needs my help. Circumstances may be such about you that I may be of use. Send for me, and I will come."

Marsden offered a trembling hand and said,— "I am sorry to hear this—but I thank you for the confidence you show in me—and it shall be as you wish. If she ever needs you, I shall send for you, Bentley,—yes, I promise, before any one else in this world."

When the white-faced and unnerved worldling departed, Bentley sat in the dusk and deepening twilight, thinking of many things, but always as they centred about Isabel Marsden. Into the falling night he lingered in thoughtful dreaming, and did not mark the darkness nor the gloom, for the happiness of loving was upon him, and his heart, which had spoken at last, stole from his love a light that illumed the night.

Hitherto his days had lacked scope and purpose, and though he had liked many women with a sincerity and faith none ever gauged, still this affection had never been fanned into a steadier or a stronger flame. It was always his misfortune not to accept but to analyze, and at last he taught himself, despairingly, to believe that the love of woman was not for him.

Yet love awaited him, as for all at every age and under every trial, though most she blesses those who seek her in the perfect flower and heyday of unthinking youth. And who will blame if she gives most bountifully to the faith which never questions nor falters when for age as well as youth she waits? For love is ever glad of the suing and never wearied, even if hailed in despair from the fogs and mists of the years, where the pilotless ship, beaten by gale and rusty with sea, gropes in the twilight for the port it might have found when winds blew fair and sunrise gladdened the adventurous voyage of life.

Bentley felt this truth now, and saw how his wasted years had lived under the sky and known no stars,—had loitered by the shore and heard no message from the sea. But the blindness was gone, and his world to-night was a symphony of faith and trust. He felt the fires of summer in his blood, and as the empurpling shadows enfolded him, he cried, exultingly,—

"I will love her forever and forever,—in this world and in the worlds to be."

CHAPTER VI.

GIBRALTAR.

WHEN Marsden left Paris in May, he was so ill that the doctors advised him to defer his departure for America until the autumn. He protested vehemently, but, as his own physicians said that he was taking a risk which nothing would justify, he grumblingly consented to obey.

He went to England, and, early in July, Bentley, who had postponed his trip to India, joined them. It gave Marsden a great deal of satisfaction to find that the Colonel had not—as he phrased it—"deserted his colors," for it was a part of the contradictions in the cynical old man's nature to have a larger faith and a deeper trust when he learned how earnestly Bentley cared for Isabel. And, though his belief was perfect only in himself, still he gave to Bentley as large a measure of confidence as his warped soul could offer, and, during these days of depressed idleness, as his opinions slowly slipped from the shores of old ideals, and left bare the shallows of ancient fancies, he confessed, penitently, the wrong he did in separating two lives so surely meant for each other. Finally, there came a time when he hoped that—all being over with him—Isabel might learn to love this man of truth and honest purpose.

In July, Marsden and Isabel went to the Isle of Wight, and, though his health improved with the change of scene, and the new interests which temporarily buoyed him, it became certain that his trouble was too seriously organic not to make the future one which would demand—as the price of living—unceasing care, and the absence of all shocks. It was not that his ailments were altogether physical, for the wounds seemed to be deeper than skill could diagnose, and, although he never confessed it, he was struggling with mental troubles, haunted by ghosts of his past, which would not, in his impaired bodily condition, yield to any treatment.

This illness and worry made him a fretful and difficult patient to manage. He had been so successful, hitherto, in his dealings with men and affairs, his brute persistency had so easily overmastered in the struggles wherein he engaged, that he was unwilling to acknowledge the weak spots in his armor. His peculiarities became intensified, and in opposing to his misfortunes what he believed to be, and called, the courage of a strong will, he arrayed against himself, by an arrogant irritation which was a form of dementia, many of his acquaintances and friends.

He soon grew tired of the Isle of Wight, and one day, while sore from a fancied slight, said to Commodore Percival, who had come to Europe for a holiday in the Black Forest, and never could tear himself from the sea shore,—

"Confound these doctors! They are all charlatans, and are simply seeking the nimble guinea of the Yankee victim. I am sure they don't know my case."

"Why don't you change them?" growled Percival. "There is no law which requires an amiable patient to stick out his tongue and present his pulse to any particular sawbones who bids him stand and deliver."

"That's all well enough for you," replied Marsden, "with your savage good health, but I must go to them. That's a part of my trouble. Now, look here, Percival, what have I done to deserve all this? Why am I cursed in this way?"

"You would not be happy in Paradise, Marsden," returned the Commodore, "nor if you had cabin duff every day for a month. You have been too long on shore, and what you need is a long sea voyage, with fresh air, nothing to worry you, plenty of exercise, and fo'k's'le grub." Percival would have prescribed the same treatment for a broken arm. "Why don't you get out of this," he continued, hoping that this last suggestion, if not the remedy, would be accepted, as for ten days Marsden had been boring him dreadfully.

"Get out of this," repeated Marsden: "why should I. The place"—he had loathed it five minutes since—"gives me, in some degree, what I want. Not that my needs are great, for my philosophy of living is a simple one: sunlight, a good dinner, sound wine, a comfortable bed, and the right to regulate my own affairs."

This conversation took place in the club-house, where both had been put up by the expansive hospitality of a member, who was, for a wonder, trying to return some of the courtesies he had received in America.

Though it was only eleven o'clock in the morning, Percival had already made it seven bells, and reporting the sun over the foreyard, was regaling himself with a brandy and soda,— "just to sweeten his bilges," he roared across the room to a retired British Rear-Admiral, who looked on envyingly at the feast which his doctors denied.

For a week the Commodore had been sailing

with his lee guns under water, waiting for a good chance to "bring up with a round turn that aggravating, money-grubbing, sour-faced grumbler, Marsden." In the audacity of the alcohol, which made him red and uncomfortable, this chance was discovered now, and, without any preliminaries, he exclaimed, brusquely,—

"See here, Marsden, I have known you since '48 or '49, when I was on the Pacific slope,— thirty years and better,—and you have always been the same. I suppose you would get angry if I hinted that you were a society of organized selfishness, so I won't; but you are, all the same."

"Commodore Percival," replied Marsden, with a face puffed out like a cream cake, "even our long acquaintance and the well-known, but indefensible bluntness, not to say coarseness, of your profession, will hardly—"

"Will hardly what?" interrupted Percival. "Will hardly justify me—of course they won't, but I do not need the justification and you do. I want to give an old sailor's advice, and I mean it kindly. Do you know everybody is growling at you, and as we would like to stick by our countryman against these constitutional grumblers over here, we are disheartened because you won't give us a peg upon which to hang an excuse. Why don't you try the other tack? Take heart of grace; bear up, man; don't you see you are killing that sweet lass who gets double rations of the sort of talk you serve out so liberally to everybody else. Hear an old friend's advice;" Percival softened when he found what a poor foe Marsden made after the first broadside had been poured in—"run up to London; put these Lime-juice doctors in quarantine and consult Jack Dalton. He is Fleet Surgeon now, and a capital fellow, with a heart as big as a Frigate's main topsail and a head loaded chock to the muzzle with sense and science. He knows more of human nature and medicine combined than any other medico who ever rammed a bolus down my throat,—and that is because he's a sailor, every inch of him, as well as a doctor. Here's my card, Marsden, and if he don't honor it, by telling you the truth, why Jack Dalton is changed and I'll eat my last commission. But you will have to hurry; he has only ten days' leave, and if you miss him I will cheerfully act as your executor."

Marsden's dignity was hurt. He strode homeward with flaming cheeks, and for days told everybody that of all coarse brutes the sea specimen was the worst. But he took Percival's advice and went to London.

Dalton, who was a prince among men, the

cheeriest of companions, the tenderest-hearted of doctors, the most loyal of friends, received Marsden with such a welcome that some of his own sunshine crept into and brightened the dark spots of the invalid's mind.

He listened patiently and agreed, as these physicians always do in their pathological free masonry, with the diagnosis of the other doctors. But his remedy was different, for he advised his patient to go home immediately in a sailing vessel and by way of the Southern passage. He gave specific directions about diet and hygiene, told just what wind and weather, and what health-giving properties of rest and tone, might be expected at this season, and altogether infused so much spirit, that the grumbling invalid began the next day to make inquiries for a suitable vessel.

Upon his return to Cowes, Marsden was so elated with the possibilities of a cure, and so garrulous and prophetic about the future, that Isabel absorbed a renewal of the courage which had almost deserted her.

She had lost something of the bloom stolen in the early spring, though this only accentuated the purity and spirituality of her beauty. She was depressed by her father's illness, and tried in many ways, not by his positive treatment of her, but by the negative sorrows which came from his strained relations with the people about him. She had never been consulted about this voyage, and had opposed no objection to what she believed to be the idea of a mind disturbed by an illness which made abnormal things look natural; but when her father returned with the sunshine of Dalton's optimism running riotously in his blood, she accepted its possibility as a blessing.

So she was much pleased, one day while looking from the pier at the yawls and cutters fretting at their anchorages, to see her father meet his old friend Bradbury, of the firm of Bradbury & Winslow, ship owners, formerly of Salem, and now of South Street, New York. The change in Marsden shocked Bradbury, and when the question of his ailments arose, as it always did with great promptness, Isabel was delighted to hear the merchant say,—

"Dr. Dalton is right, and Marsden, I have a remedy. Do you remember the Halcyon? No? Well, you should, as you own a piece in her. Just now she is loading at Genoa, and ought to be in the Straits, homeward bound, about the middle of August. What do you say? Run down to Gibraltar; I will telegraph Captain Waite to put in there, and if you are ready for the voyage, go on board; if not, the trip will have done you no harm, and the detention of the ship can, at this season of the year, make no possible difference."

Marsden growled a surly thanks, which implied an off-hand refusal, but when subsequently he learned that the Halcyon was a fine ship, half-clipper built, with a large cabin, and a master whose reputation was excellent, he accepted the offer. They went to London, and to settle definitely his intentions, passage was engaged on board the P. & O. steamer Trafalgar, which was to sail on the 8th of August.

Bentley was in London, and on the day appointed, accompanied them to Southampton. He presented to the superintendent of the fleet, and to the captain of the Trafalgar, the letters given him by old Admiral Leighton, the chairman of the company, and then saw his companions safely on board ship.

For days this parting had hung over him as an impending calamity, and he waited in a nervous anxiety, and with a distrust of himself, to speak his farewells. But, by the time the ringing bells and the rasping voices of the stewards told him the parting hour had come, he had brought himself to such a point of self-control, that his good-byes to Isabel were as calm as if he was to meet her on the morrow.

As Marsden walked forward with him, he was

very quiet, but when the gangway was reached, he said: "Well, I suppose this is the end of it; so a pleasant voyage and good-bye." After waiting a moment, he added, looking aft, where she sat watching them: "God bless her, and remember, if I am ever needed, send for me."

The lines were slackened, the rushing steam was checked, and, as Bentley went to the pier-end, and with bared head, stood among the group waving farewells, the ship steamed slowly out of the dock, amid the cheers which rang with sobs for echoes. Fainter and fainter, the Trafalgar grew, first a blurred mass in motion, next a curl of wreathing smoke, now a mist to leeward, and then —nothing. Nothing but the memory of pale faces and of glad ones, of ringing cheers and waving hands, of tear-choked voices, and of blue waters, changing to the gold and ruby of summer twilight. But Bentley saw none of these, and for him there was the remembrance only of the wistful face of his dear love, looking upon the land with longings never felt before. Would she have been happier had she known of the heart wearied with hopeless love going back that night to London's care and trouble?

The voyage of the Trafalgar was uneventful; there was a breezy night off the Needles, a disagreeable sea and half-gale to Finisterre, and such smooth water and favoring winds in the Bay of Biscay, and along the Portuguese coast, that Gibraltar was reached early on the fifth day.

Marsden was an excellent shipmate, and came out brilliantly in a new light, as the hearty, but reckless sailor. The impression made was so good, that he began to believe he was, after all, a capital, hitherto-misunderstood fellow, with a positive genius for concocting all sorts of impossibly-named American drinks, and a sublime patience for cutting in with the worst whist players in the ship. He sat at the captain's table, capped oracle with oracle, received a flattering attention from the younger men, though this last was mainly because of Isabel, and was the umpire of every game, from shuffle-board to Twenty Questions, which the uneasy spirits of the ship evolved. By the time the Trafalgar reached "Gib," as the subalterns called it, he had made a half-dozen agreeable acquaintances, among them an American named Lorrimore, who, after idling away his vacation in England, was now bound for the Rock, in the hope of catching one of the Italian steamers which touch at Gibraltar, en route to New York.

Lorrimore had presented himself on the second day out, by recalling a previous meeting in

England, and, though Marsden did not remember this, he accepted the fact much as a prince might receive a foreigner, who had done him a knightly deed upon a battlefield, where he was sorely pressed by enemies. For it was a part of Marsden's nature, under the circumstances which operated in his present environment, to assume as true what people conspired to humor as an idle whim.

The sea air, new faces and different life convinced him that the same conditions would, in a longer association, effect a cure; and when he learned that the Halcyon had not arrived, his complaints of Bradbury's neglect and unkindness were bitter indeed. A telegram received the next day did not change this attitude of despair, for the vessel had not sailed until the eleventh of August, and, with the weather to be expected at that season, might not reach the Rock for a fortnight.

"Two weeks on this hill," he roared,—"why, it's a rat-hole, a prison, and I wish I had never come. Isabel, dear, why did you let me be persuaded into this wild-goose chase, when I was so comfortable at Cowes."

He worried and fretted over this delay so much that the next day he was prostrated by a high fever and an alarming weakness in the heart action. Lorrimore was such a devoted nurse that Marsden implored him not to visit Tangiers; it was a horrible place, he growled, all fleas and crippled misery. Lorrimore agreed, willingly, to stay, but insisted that a physician should be called in.

Though the employment of simple remedies brought Marsden about rapidly, the illness had enabled him to solve one difficulty with which he had been struggling, for his first act was to send Bentley a telegram, asking if he could make arrangements to join them at the Rock, and cross in the Halcyon.

Within five hours a cordial assent to the proposition was received, together with the announcement that Bentley would sail on the seventeenth.

Marsden was a new man after this was settled, and, though he communicated the fact to no one, its effect was evident. He entered with a feverish spirit into the amusements of the place; he went at times to the Barracks, had the officers he knew best dine with him, drove about the Rock, and as far as San Roque, but no further. "No," he said, when a party was being made for a trip inland. "No! I know my Spain like a book, and it is tiresome reading after the first page. You see it all in a day. Hidalgos, onions, pride, guitars, oranges, bodégas, the merry, merry muleteer, castinets, flashing dark eyes, contrabandistas, mandolins, quick knives, Boabdil, gypsies, bullfights, *Bravo Torro*, fans, Moors, olive oil, bad cigars, and this Rock, which, by St. Jago, they have loaned to England till the times are ripe, and the larks fall. No, I loathe it, and so does Isabel. But you go, Lorrimore, or, what is better, try Tangiers. It is more oriental than Constantinople, and the best thing, by long odds, as a study of the East, this side of Damascus."

"But I have missed the steamer," replied Lorrimore, amused at the different estimate Marsden now put upon Tangiers.

"You wouldn't go in the steamer? Oh, that would be a great mistake. You would lose the preparatory appetizer. Get all the local coloring you can," answered Marsden.

"But that means discomfort."

"Ah, you have no poetry in your soul," exclaimed this Sybarite, who would not have suffered ten minutes' hardships if he had to miss the finest sight in the world. "Go across the Bay to Algeçiras, and if old Perez is alive, he will give you a place in the boat which supplies the Ceuta Garrison with cattle, and you can work your passage somehow. Put your feet in the bilge puddle at the bottom, rest your head on a cow, get as ill as you like, eat garlic with the greasy conscripts, drink the red ink they call Colares, salaam to the Grand Bashaw, buy a fez cap and a pipe, bake in the sunlight,—but return before the twenty-fifth. Go, my boy, be poetical, and go with my blessing."

Lorrimore crossed to Tangiers, and Marsden and Isabel settled down to a quiet enjoyment of Gibraltar. He spent the best part of each day reading the newest novels, and lived with the characters, no matter how unreal or impossible they might be; he was moved to tears by the sentimental chapters, and filled with joy when lowly virtue triumphed over wealthy vice; he read choice bits aloud, and generally conducted himself as a literary person of nice taste.

Isabel went in the mornings for long walks, and on band days, when Marsden could be with her, lingered in the garden of the Alameda, after the music had ceased. To her there was a charm in the quaint life of the Rock, and an unending pleasure in the contrasted people of the two continents. The grave and stately Moors returning after sunrise from some eastern point which looked toward Mecca; the British soldiers, trim and automatic; the Jews in gaberdines; the pale-brown Spanish girls with shining black hair; the yellow-gartered muleteers, driving with shrill cries the water-laden donkeys; the native women in red cloaks and hoods, edged with black velvet; and, once, a woman from Tarifa, grim with the *yashmuk*, and gaudy with bracelets of sesquins and bangles of the little sharp-pointed shells found on the Rif Coast.

Upon breezy mornings she went to the Water-Port, and watched the squall clouds sweeping seaward, the white sails of distant ships, the red and yellow boats bruising and battering each other at the landing, and the swaying of the lateens, as the xebecs brought to the mole the motley passengers from the Spanish mainland or from the dull and dead towns of the African coast beyond.

Bentley landed, one blustering morning, at this same point, tired with the constant shaking of the steamer, and wet with the spray which dashed over the bow of the clumsy boat he had hired to take him ashore. He jumped briskly to the slippery mole, had his luggage passed out, tossed the boatman a coin, and, looking about him, thought, in the joy of being near Isabel, that this was the Gate of Paradise.

But when the hotel was reached, a nervous anxiety that was beyond control dissipated the courage which had sustained him so long; and though he had not breakfasted and was as hungry as a shark, he did not venture down stairs until after ten o'clock.

Marsden was on the alert, and greeted him with a quick, glad cry of recognition, which was followed by a moment of restraint, that might have been embarrassing but for Bentley's frank and cordial manner. This reassured Marsden, who led the Colonel to a seat, and said,—

"It's a delight to have you here, though I am afraid my selfishness has put you to serious inconvenience. But the truth is, Bentley, I am convinced Doctor Dalton must be right, and this voyage is to make a new man of me. I was suffering from a bad turn when the telegram was sent, and had you not promised to come, I should be in bed this blessed minute."

"Then I am doubly glad to be here," responded Bentley, sincerely.

"Ah, my boy! that is just like you. I am all right now; but for an hour or two I feared the worst might happen. Fortunately, nothing came of it except to make plain what might occur at any time. Of course, I cannot go on board the Halcyon without my daughter, and should anything happen there,—I mean a serious illness,—it would be hard lines for Isabel to have no one in whom she could put confidence. I remembered your promise, and to cut short the whole story, I wanted you to be near. I may have been a selfish brute, but, in this, at least, I am thinking only of her."

"You did right, and I am honored by the trust you place in me."

"Thank you. But, while we are on this subject, let me be frank with you now, and confess, that of all the miseries possible in this world, none would be so serious as a separation from my daughter, at any time, or under any circumstances. Indeed, Bentley, if I dared to believe that, when my last hour came, she was not to be with me, I would have no more peace nor rest in life."

Bentley was about to reply, when he heard a light step upon the stair, and the rustling of a woman's dress. Turning expectantly, he saw Isabel, quietly and gracefully coming toward them. She was dressed in lawn, and at her throat a half-blown rose trembled happily beneath a face which, like Unas, made sunshine in dark places.

Ah! the love, the love, he gave her, and the tender eyes which gazed!

Slowly she came downward, not seeing him until at the very bottom of the stair, and then, as he stood with outstretched hand, she murmured, confusedly,—

"Colonel Bentley—and here?"

As she bowed her head to hide the glad surprise which glorified her face, the flower shrined at her neck fell to his feet. He lifted it quickly, and answered,—

"Happily, yes."

The faded petals of that Southern rose are cherished to this day, for in the time to be he learned all that this meeting had brought him.

CHAPTER VII.

HALCYON, AHOY!

THE blustering day had changed to one of sunshine and brisk breeze, the rack and squall had blown to leeward, and in the bright coolness of the morning, Bentley accompanied Isabel on her walk, and renewed the recollections of the town he had known so well years ago. They listened to the band in the Alameda, sauntered idly through the gardens, prim with graveled paths, and tortuous with a labyrinth of flaming flowers, and then strolled homeward by way of the Ragged Staff, where, all day long, noisy Scorpions harried the patient donkeys which climbed the steep incline leading from the fountain.

This was the first of other happy walks, for in its quaintness, its contrast of types, its traditions, and its isolation, the Rock had an interest which appealed at once to minds sympathetic with nature and man, and critical with the wide experience of Old World travel. When they returned to the hotel, they were aglow with the physical response of their exercise, and happy in the truer understanding of the ties which held their lives, though this was the knowledge of intuition; for, dreaming of the future, they had spoken, not of the present, but of the past.

Isabel knew nothing of Bentley's expected arrival, and after the first surprise had passed, accepted it with a happiness which confirmed the revelation her heart had made, when she saw him standing, unheralded, at the foot of the stairs. Bentley offered no explanation of his presence, and chose to assume that Marsden had spoken of his coming, though, from her startled greeting, he was certain this could not be true. She asked no questions; and he volunteered no answers to the inquiry her mind might be making, for he felt that silence would most surely prevent either being placed in a false position, at the beginning of a voyage where circumstances might solve naturally the riddle to be guessed.

Bentley had loved Isabel Marsden for nearly a year, but it was with that unquestioning affection, which governs unselfishly the springs of being without revealing the nature of the ruling force. He had missed her with longings nothing could soothe into forgetfulness, and had known content and peace only when she was near. In the disparagement of his own possibilities, he believed this was due to the separation of two natures, which, complementing each other, were in accord, and he gave no name to this desire and its completeness, until, in that moment of sorrow, when he knew it was a love, the fruition of which seemed hopeless.

Though Isabel had been happy with Bentley, she realized for the first time, when they parted at Southampton, how much he had become in her life. With this knowledge there were born longings for something lost, regrets for things done and undone, and struggles for acceptance and resignation. In the end, with the exercise of that reserve power which enables women to bow before the inevitable that men impotently deny, she schooled herself to accept this hopeless love, if not for the best, and if not to be forgotten, at least as something to be hidden, even from herself.

She would have been wanting in the intuitive instinct of her sex had she failed to see in Bentley an appreciation and a care for her which had their roots deep in the soil of a true affection; and if she could not determine where this ended and love began, it was because she did not know that both were equally hedged about by cruel bounds of circumstance. Isabel, by a promise given to her father months since—ah! how cheerfully then, and with such unquestioning faith in her strength to keep it—that no man's love should ever separate their lives; Bentley, by the acceptance of an agreement with Marsden, never brutalized by words nor penalized by vulgar compact, that in his association with Isabel he would never by word nor action seek to win her love. They were both honest people and kept these promises, fruits as the pledges were, of that selfishness which tries, with a cruel egotism, to crush the strong-eyed, sun-nursed love that ever waits and rules.

When they left Marsden that morning, he had his chair carried into a garden near the Bay, and looking upon the blue sky and bluer water, he lived over again in his past life.

It had been a strange and cruel one.

Years and years ago there was, in his days of wild adventure, one experience which he thought but few men knew. He had gone to the Pacific, even before the yellow grains in Sutter's mill-creek made in the Occident a new Republic built upon sand, but as stable as the bed rock which underlies. He had traded and mined in Mexico, and at last met and married, in a quiet, drowsy puebla of Upper California, the black-haired, bright-eyed daughter of Don Felipe del Gado, to whose hacienda he had been brought, stricken with fever and sorely jarred by travel, from the mines of the Lower Peninsula.

There was, after this marriage, a year or more of such happiness as could satisfy a nature like his in a land where the sun, blazing upon unturned fields, casts shadows only under the knarled and stunted olive trees which shake their dusty leaves to the parching breezes blowing from peaceful seas. He could not enter into the dull life about him, and not knowing its spirit nor its compensations, showed a contempt that brought him the dislike and hatred of the race with which he lived.

Swinging lazily in his hammock on the cool verandas, or riding aimlessly over the brown stretches where Don Felipe grazed his flocks, it was ever with the same thoughts,—bitter regrets for the folly which tied him to these people, useless plans and plots to escape from the thraldom of the land. But in vain; and so, through dreary months of despair, he lived in the benumbing idleness of that semi-barbaric valley.

The chance for release, however, dawned at last; for one day, with hurrying hoof-beat and the clatter and jangle of steel and brass, came the news of the gold to the northward. "Gold! by the sainted soul of Francisco d'Assis!" cried the dusty and spurred rider who hoarsely told the story as he rested, on his way to the south, in the moist, cool court-yard at noon. "Gold, Don Felipe, by the millions!—in river, in hill, in valley, in dried *quebradas!*—and to be had for the asking!"

In a week from that night Marsden had left his home forever. He had spoken to his wife of the chance this search for gold offered, even during a little absence, but she had begged him to wait, if only for a month; had sued and prayed for herself, and for the sake of the child that was yet to be. But she begged in vain, though he gave her a lying promise, and, even as he kissed her tears away, his busy mind was plotting how he should go.

And so at midnight, when the cheerless fog drove in from the sea where Cape Concepion shoves its headland into the mist and rain, he rode warily out of the olive-grove back of the house, into the spectral fields, past the farm and pastures, through the chapparal and brush and northward. As he reached a bend where the road dipped and was hidden from the home that had cured him in sickness,—from the girl who loved him as Chadizah loved,—he saw through a window facing the sullen east, the tremulous gleam of the taper which ever burned in his wife's room before the shrine of the Blessed Mother.

When daylight came, he was miles away; when night fell, leagues were between him and the moaning wife, stricken by grief with her awful agony; and, as he rode into the tent-crowded plain near the Mission of San Francisco, humming a jocund air of liberty and watching the moon's rays in the sea, there broke upon the stillness of the night in the South the first, sad wail of a child born to a heritage of woe.

When he reached the diggings, Marsden,—for he resumed the name which he had abandoned,—toiled and struggled, struggled and toiled, with the best and worst of the people about him; and if not with better luck, at least with greater profit, for he saved what he took from the earth or made in barter. Before many months he was a man of note, even in that lawless community; and with a clear head, a cool judgment, and a heart which never knew an unselfish pulsation, prospered so much beyond his best hopes that in the end he was by far the richest man in the camp.

In all this time he had never given a thought to the wife he had left behind, and she passed away, as if she had never been, in the mist which the search for gold spun around the life he had known.

But it all came back one day when a swarthy-skinned, keen-eyed native rode slowly into the valley and dismounted at his cabin. The rider was dusty and travel-stained, and his face was worn with the weariness of physical and mental strain.

When Marsden saw him, he looked to his revolver, hid a knife in his shirt, and, with a blanched face, stepped out of the hut; for this grimy, wearied rider was the man from whom he had won the daughter of Don Felipe, the one person of all the world who would have died for her.

As Pedro de Saldo dismounted he left his pistols undisturbed in the cumbrous holsters, and approaching Marsden with a face that never changed, gave him a letter, soiled with handling and sealed with crimson patches of wax.

De Saldo stood quietly awaiting some sign. When Marsden awoke from the first stupor of surprise he muttered, in a tone which was meant to be cheery, a few words of welcome, and offered his hand. But the Mexican waved it quickly aside, and said,—

"No, no, Don Henrico! They would kill me if they thought I had touched your hand."

Marsden turned to the busy camp as if looking for help, but made no attempt to read the letter. Finally he asked if an answer was wanted.

"That is for you to say, not now, but later, as I am forbidden to carry it. There is news in it for a man to study before he acts. When you are ready you will find us easier than I have found you, for I have searched everywhere in the gold camps these two months. We did not know your names in the South; but you know ours, and whatever answer you may have, send it, if you please, by messenger, to the Priest of the Mission of Santa Catalina, addressed to our Padre Dominguez."

The Mexican called his horse, softly stroked its face, and tightened the girths of the saddle. Then, with one hand clasping the stallion's neck, he said,—

"You saved me once, Don Henrico, from the stampede of the unbroken colts. I have never forgotten that, and the Padre, knowing this, asked me, of all, to find you. It will be well for you— and I advise you to remember this—never to seek the hacienda of Don Felipe again—for he, too, is dead. Be wise. Live and die here, anywhere, among your friends, with your worst enemies—but never come to *Casa Blanca*. We are a good people only where we love or honor, and they will kill you there,—*abajo*,"—he motioned with his hand and threw back his head to indicate the land he had left,—"they will

kill you,—even I would try to kill you there,
—*abajo.*"

He lifted himself in his saddle painfully, stood for a moment with slack bridle, and added,—

"Don Henrico, farewell for ever, and be wise. We have a proverb born of our land and homely ways,—listen: 'The wife's curse is the halter of the husband.' Do you understand that? Try, for it means much to you, Don Henrico, and now, *adios.*"

Marsden watched Pedro de Saldo as he rode slowly by the dry brook, up the little hill, out of the cañon, and into the brown mountains that walled the camp from the outer world, and then flung a curse at the man he had wronged.

What the letter contained he never revealed; what he thought of the news no one ever knew; for in vain, during many days, did the spurred and booted messenger of Padre Dominguez wait at the drowsy mission of Catalina. But it told Marsden that his poor wife, sorely stricken, had waited, and waited, and waited, with patient longing, with undiminished trust, until the pain was stilled, and the faith had its higher fulfillment—in death.

Weeks afterward, Don Felipe, whose light and air she had been, fell ill of a broken heart. The grim old pioneer had never spoken of the man who had wrecked their lives, but, in the last days he took such precautions as would—so he told the priest—prevent more harm coming to his blood by the treachery and cruelty of the Gringo.

He willed his property, half to the Church, and half to Padre Dominguez, to be kept in trust for the support of his daughter's child and her foster-mother. These two he sent by the long route of the land to the eastern seaboard, and thence, in compliance with the mother's last wish, to the country of her husband. But Don Felipe hid their tracks so completely, that Marsden, even had he searched, could never have found them. Then, having made his peace with God, and dictated to the Padre the few lines which told of the birth of the daughter and the mother's death, he turned his face to the wall, and, with an awful prayer for vengeance, died—as his daughter, his Carmenita, had died,—of a worn-out, wearied heart.

Years afterward, Marsden tried to find some trace of the child, but those who knew the secret were dead, and it had disappeared as one whose name is writ in water. It was to hide the memories of this past, and with some dull hope of making compensation that, five years later, on his return to New York, he had wooed and won the mother of Isabel. As he remembered all these things now, and recalled the two women who had died for him, he prayed, that by his treatment of Isabel, forgiveness might be granted him for his neglect of the child he had never known.

The days of waiting in Gibraltar passed pleasantly. Bentley had heard nothing of Lorrimore, until Marsden said, one morning,—

"By the way, I met on the steamer a young American, named Lorrimore; he is a shy, retiring sort of chap who was most civil to me. Just now he is in Tangiers, but may return at any moment. He intends sailing, if possible, from Gibraltar, and, I know, would be delighted to go with us. I have not asked him yet, though, if you do not object,—for I concede your rights in this matter,—I should like to offer him a passage in the Halcyon."

"And your daughter?" replied Bentley, in that selfishness of love which only considers how this may be affected.

"Oh, bless you! she won't care one way or another. She hardly knows him. And, as for Lorrimore, it is not a case of *beaux yeux;* at least, not of Isabel's, for he half confessed it was to escape some such affair at home, that had sent him mooning about Tangiers at this season of the year."

"I am sure," answered Bentley, "you are lucky to have found Mr. Lorrimore. By all means let him come."

When the Halcyon did not arrive upon the morning of the twenty-fifth, Marsden worked himself into such a furor of impatience, that Bentley and Isabel went, in self-defense, for a long walk to the plateau of the Signal Tower. As they came down the Rock toward noon, they saw in the Bay a trim merchant ship, slowly standing up, under all plain sail, for the anchorage. Her spars were lofty and tapering, the cotton canvas was snow white, and, as she forged ahead, her motion was as graceful as that of a bird, poised high in the idleness of a summer twilight. When she drew past their point of view, the sails unmasked the fluttering folds of an ensign, its galaxy of stars standing out against the white of the canvas, and its stripes trembling as a flame might in a calm.

They watched with eager curiosity, as, with a tumble of foam, she shot into the wind, and, in graceful curve, anchored in that safe holding ground, which lives upon the bearing between Mala and San Roque.

"The Halcyon," said Bentley,—"and home."

After luncheon, Captain Waite, of the Halcyon, called upon Marsden. He was of medium height, with the broad shoulders and sturdy frame which inspire at once a sense of confidence in a man's powers of endurance. His eyes were bright, his bronzed face was frank and handsome, and a prompt and decisive manner was softened by the cheery, mellow ring of a voice which gales had not roughened. His bearing was hearty and courteous, as he turned, with a ready smile, from one to another, and said how glad he would be to welcome them on board.

"When will you sail, Mr. Marsden?" he asked, finally; "for you are part owner, and I am under your orders."

"What hour will suit you best; for we are ready to go at any time," Marsden answered.

"Well,—how will ten o'clock to-morrow morning do?"

"Ten o'clock, let it be, and precious glad I shall be to get away," said the ungrateful invalid.

"I shall send a boat for your baggage at eight, and another one for you at nine. That will give us daylight to get well clear of the land."

"What weather do you expect?" asked Bentley. "That means a stiff breeze, does it not, Captain Waite?"

"Good weather for us, Colonel. What these people call a Levanter; that is, a fine, whole sail, easterly breeze, which will put a bone in the Halcyon's teeth, and leave a wake as straight and as white as a skate mark on the ice."

That night Captain Waite dined with his passengers, and though the change which followed sunset presaged a storm, the dinner was no less merry because of forebodings for the morrow. Waite told, in a capital style, innumerable sea-yarns—ghostly, creepy stories of uncanny misadventure, and breezy tales of wreck and rescue. Marsden came out wonderfully, and nautically, and when, at last, dinner was finished, all deemed themselves fortunate in the prospect of such congenial shipmates for the voyage.

As Waite was leaving, Lorrimore, who had just arrived from Tangiers, came into the room. Marsden had entirely forgotten him, but broached the subject of the trip, and receiving a glad assent, presented him to Waite and Bentley. When these two went out to smoke their cigars, Lorrimore laughed nervously, and said, "That was our fellow passenger, was it not? and the other was the Captain of the Halcyon? I beg your pardon, Mr. Marsden, but what did you say their names were? Colonel Bentley and Captain Waite. Thank you, one hardly ever gets a name right in these hurried introductions."

Isabel had but half caught the meaning of this scene, and looked inquiringly at her father, who explained, hastily,—

"Mr. Lorrimore, my dear, has consented to

accompany us in the Halcyon, and I am sure you will be glad to welcome him."

She spoke the graceful words her father expected, and with a courtesy which concealed the surprise and discomfort the news gave. As she was leaving the room, Lorrimore opened the door and said,—

"Thank you, Miss Marsden, nothing could afford me more pleasure than this voyage, and I hope to prove my appreciation in every way before we reach home."

At this moment the gray hill flamed with a cloud of light, and roared and grumbled with the echoes of the evening gun; the mountains and valleys took up the sound and echo, and as this tocsin of England's rule rang over the sea and land, the haughty challenge was heard with dread in the valleys and hills of the African shore; heard in the streets of Algeciras; heard on mountains and on ships at sea; and always with the maledictions of those who waited sullenly for the day when the Spaniard would come to his own again.

When the echoes died the rattle of drums, the whistling of fifes and the swinging steps of trained men, keeping time to the home songs of England, burst upon the silence, and, as Marsden went out of doors, he saw the night-guard of the

Rock sturdily marching down the crowded street. Among the hurrying throng living outside the walls, he discovered, under the glare of a street lamp, the merry face of Captain Waite, who had stopped and called to Bentley,—

"Now don't forget, Colonel, mum's the word, eh? Mum's the word!"

Marsden looked inquiringly, fumbled his cigar, and repeated to himself querulously the words Waite had used. Bentley waved his hand in answer, but as he did not offer any explanation, Marsden asked no questions, and after growling at the overcast night, returned to the room he had left.

What had happened was this. When Bentley and Waite reached the street, and lighted their cigars, the latter said,—

"Excuse me, Colonel, but do you ever attend séances,—mediums, I mean, and all that sort of thing? No. Well, I saw you took more or less interest in some of those stories I told to-night, and I thought you might be equally interested in the practical investigation. Facts, every one of them. But you don't know of any mediums here?"

Bentley was startled by this abrupt declaration, and recalled that, during dinner, Waite had dilated with curious persistency upon the subject of apparitions, materializations and spiritualistic phenomena generally. But as he was skeptical from research, he concealed his surprise, and, laughingly replied to that purport.

"So was I once, but from prejudice," answered Waite, " and I don't know but I am still, though I've seen a queer lot of things this last year, and go now whenever there is a chance, whether I understand the lingo or not; for I'm after the truth, Colonel,—yes, sir; and I'm bound to find it."

When the gun fired a moment later, and the Captain turned toward the Gate, he added,—" By the way, Colonel, don't say anything about my notions; old men and ladies get skittish over this sort of thing, and always think you are a spook or a lubber, if you acknowledge any belief in it at all."

And it was this promise which made Waite, a little way down the street, repeat, laughingly, the caution Marsden had heard.

Bentley stood upon the hotel steps smoking his cigar, and watching with soldierly interest the troops march past. The music rose and fell in the distance with remembered melodies of his war days, and, at last, in the Square by the Guardhouse, uprose the strains of that national anthem which of all prayers most surely encircles the world. When this was ended, silence fell as a mantle upon the fortress and its sleeping town; the wind freshened in squalls, and roared in the hollows of the Rock; lights swayed wearily in the rigging of anchored ships, as if begging the rest their watch denied; other lights died out, one by one, upon the rugged hillside; and in the quiet streets footsteps awoke resounding, but not unchallenged, echoes; for the hail of sentries on shore and the ringing of bells on ships in the bay, —all told of the watch the English kept by land and sea, all warned the world that though the Rock may slumber in the sullen night, its guardians never sleep.

But of those who watched and warded the crouching lion, or who on beds of sickness or of pain prayed for dawn or death, none peered with such hopeless eyes into the darkness, as one who sat far into the middle watches of the night, looking from a window of the hotel, at the ghostly spars of the Halcyon.

CHAPTER VIII.

HOMEWARD BOUND.

THE morning dawned with mist and drizzle. Clouds hung low on the mountains to the eastward, and to the summit of the Rock, and in its hollows, the fog clung like winding sheets. Feathery scud flew seaward, and heavy squalls roared in the skies, and spun in angry eddies upon the waters of the bay. The war vessels rode uneasily at their moorings off the Ragged Staff, the surf dashed in spiteful whirls over the sea-walls, and, in the Straits, now white with billows, the Levanter drove toward the Atlantic the fleet, which, for days, had been wind and current bound, between Malaga and Cape de Gatt. The white houses fringing the shore, shivered behind the mist-wreathed walls, and, under the shadow of the African coast, grey sails rolled and pitched, as they ran for a gale-blown ocean.

The Halcyon was sheltered from the storm by the anchorage she had taken, under the lee of the barrier hill; and, as she swung gently on the waves, showing her tapering spars distinctly against the sullen skies, she looked like a lily, lazily swinging in a pond of graceless weeds. Aloft, the crew were making the final preparations for sea, and in the snug cabin, the steward was busy fitting the state-rooms for the expected passengers. At half-past nine the ship's boat was sent to the water-port, and when, by ten, there was no sign of its return, Captain Waite became uneasy with a delay which might alter all his plans. He walked persistently up and down the deck, giving quiet words of command, and envying his brother mariners, who were flying westward before the favoring breeze, until, at last, for lack of other outlet, he said to the first officer,—

"Looks as if we might lose the strength of the wind, Mr. Coffin."

"Yes, sir; likewise losing time. I am all ready," replied that philosopher from Kennybunkport, interrupting himself a moment, to roar at a youngster aloft, who was seizing on some chafing gear, smooth side out. "That is," he continued, "we ain't losing as much as we may be able to spare later. No, sir'ree, not by a jug full," he added to himself, with the emphatic aphorism by which he resolved all doubts.

"Is that our boat, Mr. Coffin, under the lee of

the felucca,—the one with red and yellow bow, down there, in line with the old mole?" asked Waite, presently.

"That's our boat, sir," Coffin answered; "and the way John Johansen, of Christianstadt,—and be damned to him, for a thick-headed, North countryman,—is pulling his oar in a sea way, would be a disgrace to any ballyhoo afloat, much less this here Halcyon, and I'll let him know it!"

When the boat came alongside, Marsden was evidently in an ill-humor, for owing to some misunderstanding, he had been delayed at the hotel, and was now ready for a fierce combat of words with any disputant who offered. The captain welcomed them cordially on board, and, without further delay, hailed the forecastle, and ordered the chain to be hove short.

It was not a gay party that had assembled, for the gloominess of the day, and the depression which always asserts itself when a voyage is to be commenced, had brought about a reaction in the feelings of all, who last night had looked forward so joyously to the embarkation; but the clink, clink, of the pawls, and the rude song of the crew, as they hove in the black and oozy chain, made a music which soon revived the spirits of the company. The weather began to look more promising, as the mist rose from the land, and the sky cleared in patches to windward; and, finally, the sun appeared at times, if not cheeringly and warm, yet with that brightness which comes and goes like the shifting of a screen, when the heavens are a watery blue, and storm clouds are working eagerly to leeward.

"Avast heaving," roared Coffin, as the chain tended taut as a harp string, and straight from the Halcyon's bow to the mud-embedded anchor; and then, scampering nimbly aloft, all hands began to loosen the canvas. As sail was made, Isabel and Bentley came on deck, but Marsden, who was wet, and angry, and sorry, in his unreasonable way, that he had left the hotel, refused to join them.

With a ringing chorus, and a quavering solo, and a long, long pull, and a strong pull, and a pull altogether, the topsails were set, the yards were counter-braced, the anchor was lifted to the bow, and the Halcyon, moving like a swan, payed off to port, stole gracefully through the surrounding fleet, and, with a sturdy breeze, stood upon her course for the Straits beyond. There was a gurgle of musical water under her bows; the foam widened in sheets; the sails curved with clear cut sweep; the hull listed slightly to leeward; and the wake stretched landward in a furrow, as straight as farmer ever made. As the

Halcyon drew out from the lee of Europa Point, and caught the full force of the Levanter, the breeze was found so steady and sure, that sail was made to to'gallant sails.

They were soon in the midst of the outward bound shipping, and, as the ship overhauled and passed the dullards, the spirits of all on board arose, and they looked gratefully at the straining canvas, the trembling wind pennants, and the muscular helmsman, who swung so steadily the guiding wheel. When the anchors were stowed, Coffin came aft, and, after getting a pull here, and a pull there, till every thread of canvas drew to his satisfaction, said complacently to Bentley,—

"She's a humming-bird, Colonel; she's got the bit between her blessed teeth, and we can't hold her. She's a flyer and no mistake,—yes, sir'ree."

"She certainly is going very fast," answered Bentley. "Is this her best point of sailing?"

"She hasn't any. They're all the same, by the wind or before it, with, perhaps, a *leetle* difference in her favor, when the breeze comes over the quarter and she can carry her r'yals without strain." As Coffin looked about him, criticizing the vessels in sight, he laughed with a mechanical chuckle, and said,—

"Look at that drogher, Colonel, away off there

to the eastward; we're going two feet for her one, and before we reach Spartel, we'll leave her, hull down. Yes, sir; the Halcyon is a clipper, and just now, it seems as if all the New York girls had hold of her tow-line."

Isabel was delighted with this new experience, and such was the exhilaration of the race for the ocean, that Marsden, who came on deck, confessed it was something like sailing, after all. As Gibraltar became an indistinct mass in the distance, the sunlight glinted warmly on Tarifa, and with a moderate sea, balmy temperature, clear sky and strong breeze, the Halcyon found a perfect day. By sundown a good westing had been made, and when the departure was taken from Cape Spartel, the stars came out with the promise of a clear, bright night.

Just before the darkness fell Coffin sidled up to Bentley, and said, pointing up the Straits,—

"There she is, Colonel, there's the old drogher. I was second mate of her once, and they call her the Sea Witch. Fine Sea Witch, she is, though she's lost none of her old tricks; for there she ambles like a rocking-horse adrift in a tideway, flying our flag, hull down, and all the Daygoes, Johnnie Greeks and Dutch Galliots beating her like smoke."

The dinner brought upon the anxious steward

a shower of merited compliments; the good spirits of the captain were infectious, and Marsden so far forgot his former annoyance, as to say that he had never spent a better day in his life. Lorrimore retired to his room early, for he was a poor sailor, and when the others went on deck, it was nearly eight bells.

The night was beautifully clear, the Levanter had lost its fury, and with all sail set, the Halcyon stole like a ghost under the eternal stars. Marsden and Isabel were enthusiastic with the swift but easy movement of the ship, for accustomed, as they were, to trans-Atlantic trips on steamers, the absence of the jar and clangor of the machinery, and of the din made by the passengers moving about the decks, gave them a sense of peace and security which they had never before experienced. Marsden, with a vigorous assertion of the good hours he intended to keep, went below at nine o'clock, and left Bentley and Isabel sitting to leeward, watching the phosphorescent water and hearing the sturdy song of the sea.

Finally, she said, with an anxious questioning in her voice,—

"Do you think this voyage will benefit my father?"

"It will benefit him and all of us," he replied,

cheerfully, "for with the exceptions of the run from the west coast of South America to Polynesia, or the trip through the Inland Sea of Japan, there is nothing to compare with the southern passage, at this season of the year."

"Nothing could be better than its commencement. It has revived his spirits already, and to me it is a fairy-land,—one where the immortals sleep, and which will fade with daylight."

He looked at her with a glad smile, rejoicing in this mood, and answered,—

"Does fairy-land ever pass away? Is it not always awaiting, anxious to reveal its beauties to us, and do we not bann it with sordid cares?"

"Mine is surely here," she said, "and it is one where fairies could not live, for there is no green ring, nor flowery bank, nor opening blossoms where these good people sleep."

As he turned to look upon the encircling waters, he pointed over the starboard quarter, and added,—

"And there are its pilot stars."

As she looked, the red and green lights of a vessel, steering more to the south'ard, rose and fell in graceful salutation upon the sea. The signals grew brighter, the sails loomed in the darkness, the gear made a tracery against the sky, and as the ship passed under the stern, they saw the cheerful glimmer of the cabin windows, and heard the sturdy chorus of the watch trimming the after yards.

"What companionship there is, even in such a distant greeting as that," he said, when the ship faded in the night. "And a sad one, too, for it may be the last message of the land until we see the lights of home."

"There is a sense of companionship in it," Isabel returned, "and already I miss it as a friend—as an unknown friend, who has done in secret an unselfish act."

"Does the prospect of this isolation alarm you?" he inquired. "This thought of the loneliness which may be yours for many days?"

"No, because it is a loneliness which is never without hope. Each day, one can believe, will bring the long-expected ship, each night, the friendly light. After all, it is like life."

"Not like all lives," he said, with some little bitterness; "for to many who have tried to deserve better things, there never can be a sail on any sea, nor in any night, a light."

"That is not the philosophy of your life, Colonel Bentley, is it? You know, we agreed to accept my optimism as the truer theory of living. Confess," she added, with a smile, "that my belief is the better."

"So much better," he exclaimed, quickly, "that I have tried to disown and deny the experience, which will not let me acknowledge it is always true."

"I can understand," she said, "how men who deal with affairs, can share with you this—what shall I call it?—this doubt, negation. But what has there ever been in my life to make me believe other than I do. I have returned so little for all I have received,—indeed, I am so powerless,—that to doubt would be a treason, doubly evil for its ingratitude."

"What is the Persian proverb, done in halting verse?" he asked, smilingly,—

> "'The sun no love asks from the rose,
> The flower's life, this guerdon shows.'

You have neglected no duty," he continued, "not because it has been any easier, I fancy, except in the escape which, like most women, you have had from the experiences that prove how impossible it is to act equally by all men. Optimism is beautiful; it is a delicate flower, born of the sunshine and the dew, while pessimism is a rank weed, forcing itself in barren wastes; you expect something from the flower, nothing from the weed, even if it be a plant, the virtues of which are undiscovered. But pessimism is rugged, and coarse, and comfortable, in the freedom from care it gives to him who owns. It saves one from fatiguing enthusiasms, and furnishes arguments which can fit every individual case somewhere."

"Ah! but you must forget this creed," she insisted, "lest this isolation, which you feared for the rest of us, appalls you, even with your early sea-training."

If he could have told her that in this world there had never been a greater happiness than to sit in the starlight with her, where the world was a poem; if he had but dared whisper that with her there could be no loneliness; or if he had known that her glad faith in life was never stronger than to-night, because they were reading this story of love and life together.

He answered her cheeringly.

"No, sea-life never was distasteful to me; and I have never been fully satisfied since I left my first profession, and I have known days when its poetry was duller than any prose. The sea was my first love, to be a sailor my earliest ambition, and I have often thought the failures following my attempts at various things, grew out of the knowledge that I had begun with a mistake by resigning. Until a year ago, I was more lonely on shore than afloat, even at its worst; and I pitied no one so much as myself. It was for this I gave up all active life, and it is a truth, that when I withdrew most from men and affairs, I became most happy because I was less lonely."

"Such is the justification of the cynic, is it not?" she asked. "And I am sure you are not of that unhappy sect."

"No, because cynicism is first an affectation, then a habit. I had nothing which induced me to pose for what I was not, and I know too much of the possibilities of other men to have acquired the habit. My contentment in the world of dreams was due to other things."

"Then there is hope for you," she replied, "as there is for all of us."

"Do you think so? Sometimes I have tried to believe this,—but where is the truth?"

As four bells rang out musically, and the hail of the lookout followed, she rose to go. With an impulse he could not restrain, Bentley touched her arm lightly, and said,—

"You do not answer me. Is it because that would be asking you to give too much of your faith to one who deserves it so little?" He paused a moment, and when she did not speak, continued: "But you are right, and, perhaps, silence is the better answer."

"No," she replied, resolutely, "that would be unfair; the physician who diagnoses a disease should not be without a remedy. There is hope for you everywhere; in the world you have left, in the ambitions you have forsaken, in the ideals you still cling to, in the world you are seeking,—there, here, everywhere. But it must come from yourself, and by achievement, otherwise, it is so lightly gained that it will be as lightly lost."

He walked to windward with her, and, as they reached the rail, said,—

"Again you are right, and, at times, I have believed that I was in the road which reveals this truth, —I know it now. Let me tell you how. Once, years ago, and in some other sphere,—if you will,— when I was appalled by the failure I had made of my opportunities, an influence came into my life with the greatest good it has ever known."

"A permanent good, I hope," she exclaimed, as he hesitated for an instant.

"Thank God, yes! it is unchanging. I was wandering aimlessly, though not altogether unhappy, for I had put aside ambitions which were fruitless, and my purpose was to attain a growth, an evolution, a development, where I would find peace. This influence slipped into my life unconsciously, and gave me first, rest; next, peace; then, best of all, hope. It brought me strength to wait, to endure, and to suffer, if need be. From it

I learned how much evil my fear, my moral cowardice, and my hesitation, were working, and the faith gained from this knowledge I have not lost."

"And this influence?" asked Isabel, leaning over the taffrail to look at the gleaming water rushing past.

"Was a woman—"

"A woman!" she repeated. "It must have been a rare privilege for any woman to work such good. But she—what of her life?"

"It was to me," he answered, earnestly, "a part of everything beautiful around me; I saw it in every picture, read it in every poem. It was in the sea, in the sky, in the land, and everywhere it was pure and true."

"You will never see her again?" she asked, half sadly.

He offered his hand, and helped her carefully down the weather ladder, for the motion of the ship was unsteady enough to make these little courtesies possible; then, taking off his hat, and standing where the light from the cabin door which he opened flooded the deck, and left them both in shadow, he answered,—

"I see her always and as gratefully and happily as I see you now, for it is the truth that your life teaches which has given me my faith and hope."

She came out of the shadow, stood a moment in the light and looked at him steadfastly; then with an inclination of her head and a salutation which was so low as to be undistinguishable, she passed into the cheerful cabin.

Bentley was deeply moved by all that had occurred. He did not dare question himself as to the effect or propriety of what he had done, for the impulse had been uncontrollable and he had arrived at a stage when complete resistance would have seemed a disloyalty. He had spoken no word of love or loving, but he could not deny that he hoped she might learn how deep his affection was. In the first flush of excitement he was sure he had done only what his manhood asserted should be, but later, he was filled with dreary doubts, that, perhaps, he had said too much, or that the manner of his avowal had been too abrupt. He could justify his action in its relation to Marsden, but he feared if she should misjudge him there would be an end forever to the association which had become a necessity of his life.

He lighted his cigar, walked irresolutely for a while, went to the rail, and, without seeing anything of his surroundings, was calmed and cheered by the beauty of the night.

The breeze was fresh and pungent, as if in it were

commingled the saltness of the outer deeps and the cedar, myrrh and frankincense of the African land they were leaving; the horizon was an unbroken circle of light, and to windward, silvery clouds were sailing where the moon, in its wane, looked down upon a crescent of tremulous waves. There was no sound about the spectral decks, save where the watch gathered under the weather rail, was listening with deep interest, to the high-pitched monotone of a man-of-war's man, who was telling, as his personal experiences, the adventures of many a hero, dead before he was born. The lookout forward was silhouetted against the head stays; and aft, the second mate, new to his responsibilities, walked zealously from the wheel to the weather rigging, and looked alternately at the compass and the horizon which told only of a quiet watch.

As Bentley glanced through the cabin skylight, he saw Marsden and the captain sitting over a steaming glass of grog, and finally heard a boisterous good-night as the latter came on deck for his last look at the weather. When he saw Bentley, Waite said, and this somewhat noisily,—

"Not a bad day's work, Colonel, for a deep-laden ship, and where was there ever a finer night for getting clear of the land? If this breeze holds we will make our westing and run down for the Trades before Sunday."

"It is a perfect night and the Halcyon has done capitally," Bentley responded, cordially. "I congratulate you not only upon the ship but upon your crew. They are as neat, two-handed sailors as I have ever seen."

"None better; no sea-lawyers nor growlers among them; strong and willing, with plenty of good wishes, and both hands for ship and owners, and that is a great deal in these degenerate days of stokers."

The captain walked aft, looked at the compass, and, declining the cigar Bentley offered him, continued,—

"But they are no better for'a'd than they are aft. I have two as good mates as there are afloat. Coffin has had his ship, and there is a lot of good timber in this youngster." He called the mate, gave him some instructions for the night, and said,—

"This ought to be a lucky voyage all around, and if for no other reason than the bright eyes and sweet voice of Miss Marsden, who has brought us this good fortune at starting."

Bentley was pleased at the heartiness of this, and replied,—

"Yes, but none better than the wishes she makes for you and the ship."

"That's kind of her," returned the captain, warmly, "and I know the Halcyon will deserve her good opinion. How bright the stars are!" he added; "and look at Polaris. Really, the faithful old boy is winking with joy to see my barky, reeling off the knots for home. Sorry you didn't come below, Colonel; Mr. Marsden and I have had a jolly night. He is a clever man, with a wonderful knowledge of everything, though we do differ upon some subjects. But who don't? Well, I think I'll turn in."

The captain stretched his arms at full length, and drew in a great breath of sea air.

"There, that would win a yacht race, and as it is my night-cap, I will sleep upon it like the relief of an anchor watch."

Soon after seven bells, Marsden came on deck.

"Hello!" he said. "How are you? Still mooning?"

"Not that exactly," answered Bentley, coming back to earth by a strong pull, "moralizing."

"Moralizing! give it up, it is indictable."

"No, it was about you, just now," returned Bentley.

"About me," inquired Marsden, "that is still worse, it means conviction. How can you moralize about a poor creature without morals?"

"No, I was wondering what you were doing

out of bed at this hour, if you expected to find any health in the voyage. I heard you at six this morning, and here seven bells have gone already."

"Hang seven bells! I came up to look at the weather, and to see if everything was all right. That is nautical, is it not? I have had a delightful evening. Waite's a capital fellow, overflowing with the most considerate and unobtrusive kindness, and filled with the most interesting yarns. But he has a bee in his bonnet. Has he ever said anything to you of his séances, and the great work he is compiling."

Bentley was sorry to learn Waite had aired this subject, but he parried the question deftly, and answered,—

"Oh, that is only a sea luxury. This ship speaks for him, and in all my time, I have never seen anything better handled."

"He's a thorough seaman, I should say, though I do not know anything about it," replied Marsden; "but, bless your soul, he is daft on spiritualism. For the last two hours, more or less, he has been telling the most creepy yarns, every one with a delightful ghost, who proved some theory. He has a book as big as an unabridged dictionary, filled with proofs; and his authorities,— my head aches with them,—how he mixed them! There were esoteric Buddhists and Brahmins, Swedenborg, Mrs. Crowe, Kabbalistic Jews, Hume, Rosicrucians, Jacob Bœhmen, Slade, Paracelsus, Mrs. Hardinge, the Eddys, Pythagoras, Sergeant Cox, and all the rest of them, not forgetting the deceased and lamented Samuel Wheeler. He is a Psychic Society all by himself. Why, Bentley, his reasons are as plenty as blackberries, to prove that 'they'—as he calls the uneasy departed—are all about us."

"I suppose his sea reading is a little mixed, but," insisted Bentley, trying to remove any idea which might react by weakening Marsden's confidence in Waite, "he is an excellent navigator, and has a reputation that is not confined to the merchant service."

"Oh, don't be afraid of my misjudgment—there is nothing incompatible between sighting spooks and getting the ship's position. But, by the way, Bentley, he is awfully down on your friends, the adepts. He scorns Blavatsky, and has never heard of Éliphas Levi. He admits that many mediums are not to be trusted, but he is certain that all you Theosophists are possessed by the devil, and proper subjects for serious police inquiry."

"You do not mean he discussed Theosophy with you?" asked Bentley.

"Discussed it," roared Marsden, "he did better; he settled it, in three minutes, by the clock. But I must bring you together in a symposium, and then, look out for your spiritual dynamics."

Bentley laughed quietly, at this fanfaronade of Marsden's, and asked,—

"But don't you think it better not to encourage these discussions?"

"Not encourage him," repeated Marsden, "I would not lose him for my share in the ship. My dear boy, he is a mine of intellectual development and wonder to me. When you find a thin, long-haired, cadaverous chap, who takes in stray five-penny bits by materializing your long-lost Indian maidens, your Mr. Gruffs, and dear little Effies, you accept it as a matter of cheerful robbery; but here is a strong, beefy, breezy sailor, who is producing at sea a *magnum opus*, and demolishes in seven seconds, by his chronometer, a wonderful philosophy, which the inheritors of the Magian, the Chaldean, the Egyptian, and the Rishis, have built up—and you ask me not to encourage him? I shall do better. I shall feed him with interrogation, go with him to his séances, dote upon his materialization, and, at the proper season, turn on my dark lantern, and seize the charlatan, with all the paraphernalia, red-handed, upon her or him, as the case may be. But, I say, Bentley, it would be a bad lookout for us, if he fancied he could see, in entranced vision, five thousand miles, or, steering by the advice of a materialized Captain Cook, land us somewhere on the Florida reefs."

"You will find his navigation as right as his seamanship," declared Bentley, "and that this dallying with fourth dimensions, and his accumulation of facts relating to spiritual phenomena, are as harmless, if not so amusing, as a collection of the good things said in your old exchange."

"Well, I hope so—but, what, in the name of Benbow and Nathaniel Bowditch, is that terrific row forward? Is it a mutiny or a round-robin?—you always have those in the personally conducted sea novel, don't you?"

It was the calling of the watch below; and as the quaint and rough summons awoke the quietness of the night, and the port-watch tumbled sleepily on deck, Marsden went to his room.

Bentley waited a little while, for now that the excitement was gone, he was pursued by the fear he had said too much to Isabel; had alarmed her, perhaps, for when she passed into the light, he saw that her face was white and her eyes were blurred with tears. But he had cast the die and his heart had burst the barriers, not only with the need of showing the truth it had held so wearily and with such misery, but of telling her that she had opened for him, in his desolation, a pathway to earnest labor, without which his life would have been as nothing.

CHAPTER IX.

A DARK NIGHT.

GOOD weather followed the Halcyon. The Captain shaped a course to pass between the Madeira and Canary Islands, though he did not haul to the southward until the ship had run far enough west to avoid the calms, which at that season are often found inside of the tenth meridian. By the time the blue skies and steady northeast trades were reached, the passengers had fallen naturally into the routine of shipboard life. Everybody was sure the voyage had been a happy inspiration, but no one more than Marsden, who was delighted with the compensations in health and quiet pleasure which he received. He passed the best part of each day on deck, and evinced such interest in the novelties of ship management, that finally he ventured with airy persiflage to be oracular about principles of seamanship and wise in prophecies of wind and sea.

Isabel's relations with Bentley were unaltered;

and happy in the certainty that his fears had been idle, he accepted the conditions of his environment as idyllic. Lorrimore suffered much in the beginning from sea-sickness and from the confinement it necessitated, but when, at the end of a week, he came on deck looking pale and ill, he received their congratulations with an optimism which confessed to nothing but the pleasures the rest of the voyage promised. His days were spent alone, generally, in reading under the shade of the awning or about the decks; but though he held aloof from the others, it was not in a moody, ill-conditioned way, or as if his somewhat strained relations with Marsden included them. With his shyness he mingled a certain tact that made this quiet avoidance the apparent outcome, either of an innate diffidence or of an absorption in studies, which relieved it from the suspicion of discourtesy. He rarely began any conversation, though he was always attentively courteous, and when, by any chance, his opinions were elicited, he was found to entertain, if not hopeful views of life, at least such as did not exclude an acknowledgment that they might be open to error.

Between him and the Captain an intimacy developed which finally made his sympathy with the latter's aims so active that his reading ran entirely in the grooves of spiritualistic literature; and when Bentley half laughingly avoided further discussions upon the subject, he intimated plainly to Lorrimore that the encouragement given by him to Waite was unwise. Marsden showed but little interest in Lorrimore, and, at times, made him the target for his rough wit, but as a compensation, the others displayed a consideration which he appeared to recognize with gratitude, though it did not alter his relations with them. Whether it was that he understood Bentley's feelings for Isabel, or because of his own reserve, he never joined them; indeed, he carried this personal isolation so far, that, if by any chance, he was talking to Isabel and Bentley approached, he would offer an excuse for retiring, and, at times, so clumsily, that his good intentions rendered the situation embarrassing.

Captain Waite was indefatigable in his efforts to make the ship happy fore and aft, and more than justified Bentley's high praise. In every way he was prudent, skillful and systematic; at half-past twelve each day he marked upon a small track chart the ship's position, and when the Halcyon's run was particularly good, it was celebrated by elaborate luncheons, which were filled with surprises of sentimental sea cookery.

The Trade Winds blew strong and steady, and

when the lowest intended limit of latitude, 24° north, was reached, and the ship was pointed due west, the captain, with lifted cares, sat down to his labor upon the great work.

The days and nights could not have been more beautiful. Over the starboard quarter the loyal breeze sang joyously and true; the sunlight shone with purity from an unmarred sky; and, encircling the silvered horizon, cloud masses rose tier on tier like the foundations of a spirit land, and held the wavering light and shadow as moon rays come and go in cañons of eternal snow. The stars pulsated in a wilderness of worlds, the seas revealed translucent deeps of blue, and in unbroken undulations the foamless waves rolled silently to the tropic islands which gem their western bounds.

The happiness aft was reflected forward, and no hour was more enjoyed than that at sunset, when the "Doctor"—as the black cook was called—came out of the galley with his battered fiddle, and played for the men, in the music of the early century, merry jigs and square dances, or tender accompaniments to the negro melodies, which they sang with lusty pathos.

But the little cloud, no bigger than a man's hand, soon appeared.

On the twentieth day from Gibraltar, the chronometer stopped. Captain Waite had wound it carefully before he went on deck for his morning sight; but, in the afternoon it had ceased going, and, upon examination, the main-spring was found broken. The hands showed the accident must have occurred at three o'clock.

Waite, though sorely disturbed, mentioned this mishap only to Bentley, but it was soon apparent to everybody that something serious had happened. The Captain lost his cheerfulness, grew reserved and pre-occupied, and, at times, became despondent. "Not that it makes such a difference," he said to Bentley, "for I have nearly run my longitude, and shall haul up so carefully to the north that I anticipate no trouble. But it's the manner of this accident which worries me."

Waite's original intention had been to avoid the squalls and fogs north of Bermuda, by passing to the southward of that island, and, as the ship had escaped, so far, the revolving storms which threatened at that season of the year, he hoped no serious disturbance of his course would prevent him preserving the original plan. Bentley was not so much alarmed by the accident to the chronometer, as by the change which he saw in the Captain, and this feeling received a double emphasis, when, one evening, as they were losing the Trades, Waite remarked, despairingly,—

"Of course, you will laugh at my superstition, Colonel Bentley, but that chronometer was stopped by no mortal agency, and it is a warning of some kind. There was just such a case in one of the East India Company's ships in 1832 or 33, and though the *Singapore Castle* was saved by a miracle, the captain disappeared, about ten minutes before the pilot came on board, off the mouth of the Hoogly. Chronometers stop, and are broken, I know, and without apparent reason, but"—and here he lowered his voice—"it's a strange coincidence, that, at the same hour, two years ago, my poor wife died. It's a mystery, and, if anything should happen, I want you to remember it isn't the first warning I have had since I left New York on this voyage."

"I respect your grief and doubts, Captain Waite," answered Bentley, "but could not this—strange as the coincidence is—have been due to some mischance? You are sure you did not wind it too tight, or that some one may have accidentally jarred it?"

"Impossible! I am always careful, and besides, the room was locked all day, and no one entered it, except the steward, whom I sent for my navigator at noon, and Lorrimore, some time after luncheon, to get the second volume of a book he is studying."

On the twenty-third day, the Halcyon lost the Trade Winds. For forty-eight hours these had been decreasing in force, and hauling to the southward, and, with the light breezes which succeeded, came violent rain squalls, accompanied by vivid lightning, and threatening appearances around the horizon. At last, even the cat's-paw, that had ruffled so tremulously the face of the waters, disappeared, and for four wretched days, the Halcyon, with flapping sails and creaking spars, rolled helplessly and unceasingly upon the bosom of a sea which glared like a shield of molten lead.

When, at the end of this second day of calm, the sunset gave no hope of cooling breeze, Marsden's irritation, which had increased hour by hour, no longer repressed its expression. With a querulous insistency, he began by growling at the ship, and, as no one contradicted him, he blamed the captain for allowing the Halcyon to be lured into a "No Man's Sea," where the invested capital, so hardly earned, was, owing to bad navigation, wasted in barren idleness. "And I believe," he grumbled to Bentley, who was the outlet for these complaints, "it's all due to Waite's damned, absurd dabbling with spiritualism."

But even sub-tropical calms have an end, and on the morning of the twenty-eighth day, the ship rolled and drifted into the region of variable winds. Soon after sunrise, a wary picket of blue appeared in the distant horizon; a little skirmish line of white foam crept, crescentwise, from the eastward, then clouds, like the smoke of artillery, and the waving banners of a host, rose in the morning air, and, finally, with a rattle and roar, there came an onslaught of the wind, which made the Halcyon rush before it, as a defeated army flies.

The sense of movement, of accomplishment, gave new life to everybody, and where a moody silence had rested as a pall, and the acceptance of a misfortune which could not be escaped had deadened hope, cheery voices sang to the breeze, and prophecies of certain victory filled the ship. Yards were trimmed, sails hoisted with taut leech, and sheets hauled aft, till every thread of canvas did its share in speeding the Halcyon over the sunlit, foam-crowned sea.

Isabel, listless, and weary with the burden of many cares, came on deck during the forenoon watch, and, after scanning the breezy waters, said to Bentley, when he joined her,—

"What a blessing it is to feel the ship moving once more, to know we are not doomed to remain here forever!"

"Like a second Flying Dutchman off the Cape," answered Bentley. "No, that is over, for the calm is dead. But, frankly, our luck has been what is usually found in these waters, though I suppose none the easier to bear for that reason. Do you think I could persuade your father to come on deck?"

"Not now; though he is better already, he would not leave his room, and sent me to drink in, as he said, the energy and freshness. But the calm has really ended?" she asked.

"Yes, the worst is gone, for even a gale is not so bad as a calm. One may burn our lives, but the other reaches the same end by rusting them. What is better now, we are heading well to the north'ard, and laying our course."

For the past week, save for the rough navigation required, Captain Waite had left the management of the ship to Coffin, and accepting the calm as inevitable, seemed to take an interest only in his book, and in trying to decipher esoteric triangles and squares, which Bentley, sadly enough, recognized as the mystic symbolisms of a form of spiritual research, to which Waite could not bring the training nor opportunities even of the veriest neophyte. When the breeze was found, the Captain simply gave the course to be steered, and, to avoid further interruptions, entered his room and locked its door. Fortunately, Coffin assumed a wide liberty of interpretation in his instructions, and before noon the Halcyon was reeling under the breeze with all the canvas she could comfortably carry.

About seven bells, Coffin said to Bentley, "'Pears to me, Colonel, she's going some, laying her course, too, with a little to spare, and knocking off a good ten knots, or I'm a howling cow-boy." After looking around the horizon with half-closed eyes, he added, " She's scoffing latitude, too, and I think the wind is sure to hold, with too tight a grip, perhaps, for down there to the south'ard it looks as if we might have a change of some kind. It will bring more squalls, anyhow, for we're just about inside of hurricane latitudes, I reckon?"

"Yes, these are hurricane regions; we are where the first branch begins to curve, at this season— but the laws of cyclones are fairly well-known, and the ship is staunch enough—eh?" Bentley replied, half questioningly.

"The Halcyon is as staunch as wood and iron and copper and good locust trunnels can make a ship, and the Captain, he's a prime hand for tackling cyclones—knows all their dodges, that is," Coffin continued, lowering his voice and looking about cautiously, " used to know, and does now if nothing has gone wrong."

Bentley, who understood Coffin's meaning, took

two or three turns on the deck, and asked meditatively,—

"You notice a great change, then?"

"I've sailed with him off and on for twenty years, deep-water voyages and all, and learned what I know from him; but he's not the same man, and hasn't been the whole voyage. No, sir'ree, not the same John H. Waite, who was the best-found and smartest master-mariner out of the Port of New York. He's been queer on this point of spiritualism ever since his wife died, two years gone this month; but he's been worse this whole voyage. No harm meant, Colonel, but couldn't you freshen the nip of his memory—he's got responsibilities and here's an owner on board. I don't like the look of things, sort of feel it in the air and in my bones, as if something was brewing, and we might get it, before night, right butt-end on and the size of a regular ring-tailed snorter of a blow."

Bentley promised to do as Coffin wished, and after this kept as close a watch upon the navigation as he could without exciting comment.

The fears of the mate were not verified; as the Halcyon, except for a rain squall or two in the dog watches, ran along speedily and with good weather all that day and night. The barometer was high, the wind dry and bracing, and the atmosphere very transparent. By noon of the next day she had logged one hundred and eighty-six knots, and the captain's reckoning put her about one hundred and eighty miles E. S. E. of Hatteras.

Between two or three o'clock Bentley noticed a sudden fall in the barometer, and soon afterward there were unmistakable evidences of a change; the upper regions of the sky grew dark, the soft cirrus clouds gave place to a veil of white and feathery mist, which spun in a ghostly aureole, the air became humid, and the heat oppressive. Before two bells in the first dog watch great plumes of gray and white waved above the sea, and to the northward and eastward a nimbus cloud brooded. The threatening appearance of this storm-bank was indescribable, for it seemed as if, in its slowly developing but irresistible path, it would enfold everything with nameless horrors; its upper part was formed of rounded and cone-shaped clouds, from which scud and squall whirled angrily in all directions, and its base, black as the Arctic night, was hidden with suggested terrors below the horizon. Presently it began to rise until it reached the zenith, and then with a downfall of rain, as if the flood gates were loosed, it dominated the heavens. The water was a sickly green, the sun set in a band of coppery sky, and as the twilight was blotted out by the angry cloud, the gale whistled mournfully, rain squalls tore to the right and left, and the sea, broken by opposing wave crests, swept turbulently to the gloomy south.

No one slept that night.

At two in the morning the wind was blowing a gale from the southeast, and when the gray dawn faintly lighted the tossing sea, the wind shifted in heavy squalls to the eastward. As Bentley entered the cabin to get his coffee, he met the Captain looking wild-eyed and dishevelled, for he had passed the night on deck or in the cabin, pouring over his mystic books. He addressed Bentley abruptly, though his tone was composed. "From my reckoning, Colonel, and from what I have learned in other ways," —he added this hesitatingly,—" I put the ship about here." He pointed out a place on the chart over one hundred miles to the eastward of Hatteras, and continued, "I have worked back, and, as you know, the log-lines and glasses have been verified; we have been careful about her logging, and so I am reasonably certain of the position; but, would you mind running over my calculations?"

Bentley took the log-slate, and working up, independently, the dead reckoning from the noon of the day before, arrived substantially at the same result as the captain.

"Well," said Waite, with renewed confidence, when Bentley gave his result, "that being the case, we ought, by noon, to be about here," and, measuring off the distance with the dividers, and shaping a course with the parallel rulers, he pricked upon the chart the assumed place of the ship. "That, you see, gives us plenty of sea-room. To me, this blow looks like the beginning of a cyclone, and, if it is, I shall try and take advantage of it; of course, I cannot tell exactly in what direction it is moving, but, from the shifting of the wind to the left, I think we are in the manageable semi-circle, and out of its direct path."

There was no doubt in Bentley's mind that Captain Waite had determined correctly the character of the storm, and, so far as could be expected, his position in it; so he replied, cheerfully,—

"I am sure you are right, and we have both seen too much of this sort of thing to fear any danger."

"I am glad you agree with me," answered Waite, "for I have been studying this threatening storm as carefully as I can, on insufficient data. But all cyclones are dangerous, and this may be what I was warned of at Genoa; the danger I was to look out for on the voyage home."

"But, and pardon me, Captain, for asking you, are you sure that the assumed longitude is right?" asked Bentley. "You know dead reckoning is not always reliable."

"Doubly sure; so sure, that I would stake my life on it," he answered, sternly.

"And you would not stand off shore a little longer, until you could get some observations?"

"No, for I know Mr. Marsden is already dissatisfied with the length of the voyage. There is not a chance that we have overrun our logging—this I know, and in more ways than one. Besides, if this is a cyclone, we might run into its centre."

When Bentley reached the deck, he found both the mates on watch. Coffin was standing by the weather-rail, carefully conning the ship, and Niles was stretching life-lines along the main deck, for the sea was heavy, and the ship was pitching and rolling viciously. The sky was a dirty gray and washed-out black, save where the whitish arc, which had formed in the east, was warmed into a mass of lurid red vapor.

Bentley called Coffin to leeward of the mast, and said, in as low tones as the howling of the gale permitted,—

"The Captain is better, and I think the time for decisive measures has not arrived; but, be ready at any moment, and, in the meantime, if there is a crisis, Marsden will put the management of the ship in your hands."

Coffin, who had not taken his eyes off the tugging and straining topsails and trysail, nodded his head in approval, and walked to windward. About noon, the weather was so much worse, that he sent for Bentley, and said,—

"There is no use in going on any longer this way, Colonel; I know as well as you we're not sure of our position, and ought to be laid-to, with our head off shore instead of trying to run north; or, for a while, to take the wind on the starboard quarter, and get clear of the storm circle. I have suggested this to the Captain, but he says it's not time for either plan yet, and what's worse, he declares he is waiting for the proper permission. The truth is, he is not right, and, though it looks like mutiny, if Mr. Marsden gives the word, I will take charge, under his orders."

Bentley knew how strong must be the impulse which lead an honest man and a true sailor, like Coffin, to prescribe such a desperate remedy; but he felt that the mate was only doing his duty. Before he could frame an answer, Waite came on deck, and ordered all hands to be called.

At this time, the ship was heading about North, on the starboard tack, the gale blowing between East and E. N. E. As soon as the people were at their stations, the Captain waited for a smooth time, and, putting his helm up, wore ship to the westward, and brought the Halcyon on the port tack, with her head about S. by E. The evolution was performed in a thoroughly seamanlike manner, and, though the wallowing of the ship, when she fell off into the trough of the sea, was so great as to bring Marsden and Lorrimore into the cabin, with nervous premonitions of danger, still the smiling face and cheery words of Bentley, reassured them.

Sail was gradually reduced, and, as the Halcyon was laid-to, her splendid qualities were manifested, in the ease with which she met the seas that, before, had made her stagger and reel like a drunkard. At four o'clock, the wind was blowing a violent gale from E. N. E., and by sundown this had become so heavy, that all the square sails were furled, and the ship was lying-to under her storm main trysail only. At eight o'clock, she was struggling desperately in the full fury of a hurricane, which rushed madly from N. E., and so mercilessly did this rage, that her starboard beams were under water, and, with a fast drift to leeward, she was wreathed by spray that dashed in white sheets over the bow and broke aft in blinding torrents.

About nine o'clock, the gale lulled for an interval, and there followed a few moments of sudden calm, so disquieting in the horrors it seemed to foretell, that, even the previous roaring of the cyclone was less terrible. The ship rolled violently in a confused sea, which boiled around her; the tops of the waves were sheared by an irresistible force, and engulfing them arose the walls of black clouds, and the skies that appeared to rest upon the mastheads. Then, with a roar, like the shooting of a thousand thunderbolts in a clear sky, the gale, without the slightest warning, shifted to the northward and westward.

As the Halcyon slowly staggered upright, to face this new onslaught, a heavy sea boarded her over the weather-bow. With cracking timbers and ripping bolts, the forward bulwarks were battered into fragments, the galley was gutted and unroofed, the forecastle stove-in, and a life-boat swept to leeward. The spare spars and water-casks were torn from their lashings, and started aft with such fury, that several of the crew, caught in the wreckage, were seriously injured, among them,

—and so badly, that he died in an hour—the kindly-hearted negro cook. The Halcyon shivered and reeled under the blow, and, when it seemed she would never right again, rose slowly on the following wave, and painfully freed herself from the tons of flooding water.

As soon as he saw the immediate danger was past, Bentley rushed to the cabin, and found that little damage had been done, though the water was slashing from port to starboard, and forcing its way, in a slow stream, through the lee scuppers near the pantry.

Marsden called Bentley into his room, and muttered, hoarsely,—

"What do you think of all this? I mean the weather, and our chances?"

With the usual caution of sailors in speaking to landsmen, Bentley replied,—

"It is a very heavy gale, but not dangerous; that sudden shift was, I think, its culmination."

"Where do you make the ship to be?"

"By the captain's last reckoning, we were one hundred miles from Hatteras; since then, we have drifted to the southward, and off shore."

"Tell me frankly, Bentley: is this a cyclone?"

"I think a cyclone has passed us, though at no time have we been out of the manageable semicircle, as it is called."

Marsden seemed better satisfied, and asked Bentley to let him know before midnight the exact state of affairs. By eleven o'clock, the wind had hauled around the compass, and was blowing heavily, but steadily, from the East, and there was a continued rise of the barometer, succeeding the slight change that had preceded the cyclone's fiercest attack two hours before.

Waite, who kept the deck, was nervously walking between the mast and the weather-taffrail, as more sail was set, and, finally, said,—

"Mr. Coffin, call all hands; we must lose no more time. I am going to wear ship."

The Halcyon was put about, and, having been brought well up to the wind, on the starboard tack, with her head North, sail was gradually made to fore and main lower topsails, double-reefed foresail, forestorm staysail, and main trysail. Coffin and Bentley did not approve of this change, but, at the worst, it was only a difference of judgment, in which the captain might be right.

Bentley went to the cabin soon afterward, and was followed by Waite, who sank wearily in a lashed chair, and said,—

"It has been a hard blow, but I think we have weathered it. I shall run on this course till daylight, for we have plenty of room, and are well clear of the Gulf Stream; then, if the storm has not broken, I shall put her head off shore, until I can get a decent observation."

Lorrimore, who had not left his room since eight o'clock, slid along the wet cabin floor, and asked,—

"Shall I be in the way on deck; it seems haunted down here."

"Haunted?" the captain cried, "haunted, yes, but not as up there. Go, if you will, though you are better below, where the lamp is."

When Lorrimore had taken his pallid face and burning eyes into the night, Waite said to Bentley,—

"I suppose you think I have not shown a proper knowledge of these storms, and that I should have run off with the wind on my starboard quarter, until I could work around, or get into smooth water. But I was afraid of being squeezed between the cyclone's track and the coast, or shoved into the Gulf Stream, which would have confused my reckoning, and so I have done as my judgment told me was best."

As he rose, and went toward the cabin door, he said, brokenly, in a voice filled with a misery and sadness which haunted Bentley for days,—

"It has been a hard gale and a dreary burden in every way, for at times my reason has struggled against my warnings. But I am only the creature of fate, an instrument for some purpose, a punishment for some sin. Why? Who can say? Thank God, the morning will make all things plain."

With a sudden impulse, he came to Bentley, and grasped his hand.

"If I could only tell you what I have suffered in these last days, you would pity me. There is a higher power than man's in all this, and, believing as I do, I have tried only to perform my whole duty."

He groped his way by table and bulkhead to the door, and then passed quickly, as the shadow of a blown-out light goes, into the gloom of the gale and night.

Bentley entered Marsden's room and found him staring with sleepless eyes into the darkness. At his request Bentley lighted the night-lantern, and, omitting the hallucinations of Waite, told all that had occurred. The invalid listened intently, and said,—

"I am glad it appears more promising. I own, Bentley, I am nervous to-night, and must ask you not to leave me just yet, as I have something to say."

Marsden looked pale and old. The corners of his mouth were drawn with a suggestion of repressed pain, his nose was pinched, his unshaven face had a two days' stubby growth of fluffy gray hair, the pupils of his eyes were dilated, and his hands and the muscles of his face twitched nervously; when he was not gesticulating, as was his habit, he held the ring finger of the left hand tightly clasped in his right.

He did not speak for a few moments, and when he began, it was in a low, hoarse rumble of throaty words.

"Bentley, if anything should happen,—not only now, but at any time,—you will look out for my daughter, will you not? I mean, at all sacrifices. I have been thinking seriously of many things, and, if not too late, I want to make such restitution as is left to me. This is not," he cried, with the old defiance of creed and dogma other than the belief in himself and the rule of life which centralized him as the only certain fact in the universe,—"this is not, from any fear of what may happen,—for as I have lived a heathen I shall die one,—but because I realize there are debts which I owe, as I would owe for a dinner I had eaten. One of these expiations is my treatment of you."

Bentley tried to calm him with words of grateful acknowledgment, of considerate kindness, but the stricken old man, eager with the desire of doing at last something which did not include himself in its rewards, went on with easy words,—

"If it is any consolation to you, as it is certainly a relief to me, let my say, that I was purblind in the foolishness of my vain interference,—but now you are free to win Isabel when you will."

Marsden lifted himself painfully from his pillow, and taking down a small tin box from the shelf above the locker, handed it to Bentley, and said,—

"But there is a greater expiation due than yours. I can not sketch to-night even the rude outlines of the story, but you will find it among other papers in this box. This restitution has to do with one chapter in my life, which, in your new relations, you have the right to know."

He spoke slowly, and turned his face with a shudder from the air-port, where the water dashed, as the Halcyon sank in the hollows of the wave.

"Years ago, and in California, I was married. I was only a boy at the time, and unfitted, by the life I had led, for any such responsibility. The marriage was a foolish, mad impulse, but, in the end, a sad one for the woman who had trusted me. After a year or more I deserted my wife, at a season when even the brutes are kind, crazy with the hunger for wealth and unreasoning in a resentment—of which Heaven knows she made no part—against a life that was throttling me. There was a daughter born, and I feel it was the last blow to the misery I had made, that my wife died without seeing me hold the little child whom she had prayed would wed our lives in the love which neither priest nor pity had saved.

"Carmenita, my wife, died as she had lived, a good, true, woman, who deserved a better fate, and with her last prayers for me and for her baby.

"Those prayers have been my Nemesis. When I awoke to a realization of my cowardice, I searched everywhere, but never could find this child, for her grandfather had sworn this should be my punishment when youth and folly were gone; and that curse, hissed at me from a hopeless death-bed, has followed and struck often, but never so cruelly as to-night. I ask your aid to make this expiation, for I am old and sick. Will you help me to undo the wrong?"

Bentley said, slowly,—

"As I love Isabel, I will try to solve the mystery of her sister's life and death."

"Should she be alive," Marsden muttered, brokenly, "tell her of this repentance, and bring her to the home and love she has, doubtlessly, never known. If she be dead, bury her by the side of the mother who died for her—and me. I owe something to Catlin; let his body be brought home, for however wrong he may have been, he was sick and poor and human, and I did not do my duty by him. At least, I might have saved him from hunger and the prison walls. And for the other—that wretched woman who came into our lives for no harm we had done, for no reason that will ever be revealed—let her memory be forgotten and forgiven: it will be a charity."

Marsden sank wearily in the narrow berth, and, after muttering a half-framed sentence, begged Bentley to bring him a glass of water. As he crossed the dreary cabin, the Colonel saw, under the swaying, smoking lamp, the sleeping figure of Lorrimore. His pose was one of utter prostration, but, as the pallid face, resting upon the outstretched arms, was turned from the vibrating circle of yellow light, it bore a look of tenderness which Bentley had never seen before. Going first to Lorrimore's room, he took a blanket, and wrapped it gently about the tired sleeper.

Marsden sipped the draught Bentley had mixed with whiskey, and, when his mind reacted under the stimulant, raised himself in the bed, and continued—

"Tell me, Bentley, what did you ever learn of her history—of Marion Darlington?"

He spoke the name with an effort, for so completely had he tried to put her out of his life, since the night in Paris when he shrank beneath the hatred of her dying message, that, at his request, Bentley never mentioned her.

"Catlin's sister," said Bentley, "wrote me all she knew, or could discover, and it was sad enough. I will show you the letter to-morrow."

"No, no!" Marsden cried, "tell me about her to-night, and we will try, hereafter, to forget her."

"Much of her story," responded Bentley, "was true. She loved Catlin, as only these grave, quiet women, can love, and, for a time, they were engaged to be married. But all this, by slow degrees, ended when he met Isabel. With this change, her nature seemed to alter, and, after a season of dreadful illness, she came back to a life which had only one purpose—to win the love she had lost. Little of her early history is known. She had a modest income, which was paid monthly by a Catholic banker in New York, until she came of age, when the principal was given her. It was, he said, a trust left by one whose name could not be revealed. Her life must have been a sad one, for her earliest remembrances, as she told Miss Catlin, were of strangers, and of harsh, unhomelike, religious schools; and she had hungered for a kind word—for some one to love her—but none of these ever came until she met Philip."

"Poor girl, poor girl!" exclaimed Marsden; "perhaps, after all, we have misjudged her."

"When I sent the news of her sad death, Catlin's sister sought the banker, and asked his advice as to her burial. Then, for the first time, it was learned that her name was not Marion Darlington, but Maria del Gado."

What terror had stricken the night? What echo of perils passed was here? What judgments were to come? What was the sudden agony which pierced this stricken cynic with spears, and filled his mouth with the mist of wine and hyssop.

"Maria del Gado!" he gasped. "Merciful God! and her grandfather?"

"Was Felipe del Gado, of Casa Blanca."

"My God, my God, whom I have denied, pity me! Oh, Bentley, Bentley! the child I left with strangers, the woman who died alone, whom I killed—she—she was the daughter I never knew —she was Isabel's sister."

Bentley put his arm about the fainting form, and slowly lowered it to the narrow bed. Into the worn face an ashen pallor was creeping, and in the wearied eyes was burning dim the light of the tired soul, which had striven so long between the sins of this incarnation, and the ambitions of the spirit, waiting now so eagerly for its æons of rest, and for the judgment of God.

With one last effort, life seemed to come full-flooded to the dying penitent, but it was the useless flutterings of a netted bird in the grasp of the fowler. Pressing a hand to his raging heart, he shrieked,—

"Help me! help me! for God's sake! My daughter, my Isabel!"

Bentley rushed to the opposite room. A quick knock aroused Isabel, and she answered with a tenderness born of the dreamland, wherein they had been walking happily hand-in-hand together. But, before he could utter a word, a cry of awful misery mingled with the roaring of the gale, and awoke, with sudden start, the sleeping Lorrimore. Guided by the moans which followed this supplication for help, he entered Marsden's room, just as Isabel sprang into the cabin, and, with the life-blood choking her heart, turned affrightedly to Bentley.

"Your father—come!" It was all that he dared to say.

When they entered, all was still, and, by the dimly-lit and spectral bed, Lorrimore, with outstretched hand, bade them stand; and then, pointing to the eyes, which were staring sightlessly into the gloom, he whispered,—

"It is too late—too late! He is dead!"

So Henry Marsden died, and, as the doctors had feared, by the shock which the culmination of all these miseries gave. The Sybarite found the treasure which the Stoic said not all the world could rob him of—the treasure of death—here where life itself was a tragedy and earth was denied him.

Oh, vain purpose, vain prayer, of this misspent life! Not upon the daughter he loved so well did his dying eyes look, nor was the touch of her hand upon his paling cheek, when the end came; not with his prayer's fulfillment, nor with his sin's expiation; for, as the peace of the passing away stole into his soul, as sleep after labor, his clouded vision saw only the face of a stranger.

He died at midnight, and the answer to his cry was the muffled echo of the Halcyon's bell, ushering in the grief-stricken day and ringing, storm-smitten, above the requiem of the gale.

But with the chime of the bell, the roaring of the blast seemed stilled, and, then, a shock, unheard, unknown before, thrilled the Halcyon from stem to stern, from truck to keelson; and, above the flapping of splitting sails, the battering of falling spars, and the rending of broken bulwarks, above the challenge of sea and gale, and the anguished cries of men, there was borne on the wings of night another message of death.

For the Halcyon's days were done, and, with bursting seams and riven timbers, she settled slowly into a grave of sand, and opened, as if pleading for pity, her gaping wounds to the seas, which wrecked her on the treacherous shores of home.

CHAPTER X.

STOUT HEARTS.

THE Halcyon had sailed her last voyage. The waves which had enfolded her keel, the breezes which had wooed her sails, the skies which had piloted her by day and night—all had conspired to kill her in the end.

After the first cry of the watch, all other sounds were lost in the gale which had hunted so hard and run down so surely this harmless quarry; but now there burst upon the night the roar of breakers which scaled the crumbling bulwarks, and rushed aft with lips of foam to riot insanely in the harvest death had planted for their reaping.

Bowed by the weight of her sorrow, Isabel failed to realize the meaning of this new disaster, or welcomed it as a solution for the future which was so hopeless. Lorrimore dashed wildly into the cabin, and then on deck, while Bentley took from the rack a life preserver and secured it about the moaning woman, who knelt by the bedside of her father.

Closing the sightless eyes and covering the body with a sheet, he whispered a word of hope to Isabel, and then made his way to the deck above.

It was a scene of misery and ruin.

The firm settling of the hull, the resistance it offered to the onslaught of the sea, and the strength and persistency of the breakers, told his trained eyes that the Halcyon was doomed. She was imbedded in the shallows for her whole length, and, as she lay slightly heeled to port, with the starboard broadside opposed at a small angle to the wind, the waves poured in torrents over the bows, rending bulwarks and houses and driving aft and to leeward a mass of dangerous wreckage. The light spars, carried away by the first shock of the grounding, hung up and down the topmast and lower rigging, or trailed alongside in a tangle of gear, which let them surge upon each wave to act as battering rams against the frames amidships.

Bentley climbed the starboard mizzen rigging, and peered into the darkness for a signal of hope or rescue, but in vain; and though he waited until their last rocket blazed over the water, it illumined an arc where only the rolling waves, the whirling foam-crests, and the pools of floating spars and top-hamper, shared the hopelessness of the situation.

At first the blows of the breakers had not been unlike the buffetings of the sea when the Halcyon was battling with the gale in the open, but now each assault made the vessel tremble in every timber, and forced from their fastenings knee and frame, beam and futtock, plank and bracing. Fortunately the Halcyon was strongly built with seasoned wood and honest men's honest iron work, so at the worst she might be expected to hold together for a few hours more.

Bentley looked for the crew, but it was not until his eyes grew accustomed to the blackness of the night that he saw under the weather rail a little group of silent men. In this were the mates, and, as Bentley's figure showed against the background of the rigging, Coffin carefully worked his way aft. When he reached the shrouds, the mate said, with his usual composure,—

"Oh, that's you, is it, Colonel? How are you? Glad to see you. Well, it's pretty much what I feared, and a bad business, too, yes, sir'ree—a bad business for all hands."

"Where is the captain?" asked Bentley.

"We don't know. I've been everywhere I dared to go, but can't find him; and the chance is the old man has gone overboard. Peterson, there, whose lookout it was, saw him when the ship struck, standing by the head stays, and talking or singing loudly; and he reckons, Peterson does, that the first sea which boarded us and carried aft the eleven who are saved, swept the captain overboard with the rush of falling spars."

"Where do you suppose we are?" inquired Bentley.

"That's hard to tell exactly, but somewhere between Hatteras and Cape Henry. You see, Colonel, this is a bad beach along here, and what with our over-running in the Gulf Stream, and the gale, and the unsartin reckoning, we may be anywhere along the coast."

It was characteristic of Coffin, that in this partial enumeration of the causes which had led to the wreck, he did not include the most potent; for with the uncertain position of the ship, the Captain's decision to stand North, instead of keeping off-shore until the gale broke or daylight came, was the real reason of the disaster.

"It is a bad stretch of sand all along from the Virginia Capes to Winyah Bay," Coffin continued. "We may be on the outer shoals of Hatteras, or, if we got more northing in the Stream, we may have struck on the Wimbles, off Chickamicomico, and then, again, we may be plum on the beach off Kitty-hawk, for right there you carry deep water straight up to the shoals without warning."

"The gale seems moderating," suggested Bentley.

"Yes, the wind is less, but the breakers are doing the work. I haven't lost my courage, but it looks, Colonel, as if we are pretty well done for. There aren't a dozen people to a quarter section on this beach, and Congress says the nation is too poor to keep the Life-Saving Station open all the year round. The country ain't got surplus enough for that, and a few sailors, more or less, don't count as voters. There's not a harbor in the whole stretch, from the Inlet to Chesapeake Bay, a hundred miles as the crow flies."

"How many boats are left?" Bentley asked, because he knew so far as human life might find a refuge, that the ship could not hold out long after daylight; certainly not with any assurance which could tempt them to await a hope of relief from the shore. The bowsprit had disappeared, and the foremast was so sure to go by the board, that the destruction caused by its ripping and tearing would give an entrance to the breakers which nothing could resist. It was useless and impossible now to cut the mast away, and their only hope lay in speedy escape.

"There are two boats," answered Coffin, "both good ones, even for this weather, but we can't launch them with this sea, making a clean breach over us, though, by good luck, all that 'ere top-hamper has fallen to wind'ard."

"If the ship would hold till daylight, the shore people might do something, but both are poor chances," said Bentley, "and I believe our only hope is in the boats. But," he added, quickly, "you are in command, and I will obey your order cheerfully."

Coffin thought a moment, slipped down to leeward, went a little way up the mizzen rigging, and looked at the sea. Bentley followed him to the rail, and when the mate descended, showed where the ship made a lee amidships, and urged that with good luck the boats might be gotten overboard safely.

Coffin answered, "You're right, Colonel; it is our only hope; the old barky is going to pieces fast, so we'll have a try at the boats. There is a fighting chance and we're just the ones to take it."

Bentley watched admiringly the hardy seaman as he pulled himself by the life-line to the bulwarks, where the men were gathered; and through the gloom, as the breakers retreated to gather strength for another sally, he saw the group quickly, and with new hope, rush and slide to leeward of the house on which the boats were stowed. Though a hazardous duty, it was undertaken cheerfully, for as Bentley descended to the main deck, he heard the ringing cheers of the sailors, as they worked with a will under Coffin's skillful direction.

When Bentley entered the cabin, Lorrimore was sitting upon the table perfectly self-possessed and stolidly whittling a piece of rounded wood, —the plug of a water-breaker apparently, which must have been washed aft in the litter floating about the deck.

"A cool hand that," thought Bentley, "and, I am afraid, an unfeeling one." He said aloud, "Mr. Lorrimore we are going to abandon the ship and the crew are trying to launch the boats. You had better make, at once, the preparations you think necessary, and then stand by to leeward."

Lorrimore raised his eyes from the shining knife blade, though without stopping his work upon the curious little block, and answered, courteously, "Thank you, I am ready now."

Bentley hesitated a moment, as if in doubt, before he entered the room where the dead man lay. In her awful vigil Isabel's head rested upon the bosom of her father, and she was still sobbing with a grief which found its only expression in low moans. He lifted her gently to the camp chair standing by the bedside, and said,

"God help and pity you, for I know what this all must mean; but he is happier and better, for all is over for him, all the strife and fear,—all the trouble and pain. He has found the peace which all our lives must seek."

She could not answer, though his pity and consolation were her only refuge now. "There is a duty you owe to him and to yourself, for you are powerless here," he pleaded. "Will you not come with me? You may trust me, for in his last moments I promised to save you at all sacrifices. Help me keep my word with the dead—with your dead and mine; for with his dying words, almost, he gave you to me, and here with the same death everywhere about us, I can tell you that—I love you."

She rose from the chair, and, lifting the shrouding sheet, kissed the pale lips, and then in silence went into the cabin with him. As he was leaving her, Bentley said,—

"The ship is stranded—where, no one knows, but if we can launch the boats we are not without hope. You will be brave, and, for his sake, bear up in these awful moments. If we are to die, it shall be together; if we are to live, let it be my right to save you."

But she made no answer, for his words gave her no realization of the perils encompassing them. All she knew was the agony of her father's loss and the utter loneliness to which even death could add no new terrors. Unconsciously her head fell upon his shoulders, and, in her need for help and strength, she wept as if her heart would break.

"He was so good to me, so good to me," she sobbed, "and now he will never know how much I loved him."

Bentley encouraged her with tender words, told what preparations she should make for the desperate trial before them, and, leaving her, went to Lorrimore, who had now entered his room.

"I will put Miss Marsden in your care, Mr. Lorrimore, until I return. The ship's danger is very great, so great, that this may be our last night on earth; but whatever the peril may be, it is not immediate. Can you trust me not to desert you, and will you remain here unquestioningly until I return?"

Lorrimore twirled in his thin fingers the little plug he had shaped so idly, and answered, "My trust in you, Colonel Bentley, is perfect, and I shall remain here until your return."

Lorrimore blew vacantly through the hole he had made in the centre of his piece of whittled wood, and twirled it by the strings, which, with curious interlacings, he had fitted in grooves about its edges. He seemed to do this as if his mind were wandering with aimless purpose, though suddenly he added, as Bentley left him, "And here is my hand upon the promise. Trust me, and, if your services are needed elsewhere, do not come until the last moment. It will be dreary watching for her, alone, with the dead."

Lorrimore's hand was cold, and it trembled in Bentley's grasp, though these were the only signs which showed he knew the misery surrounding them. He waved a salute to Bentley, as the latter was leaving, and, then, as proof of his pledge, crossed the cabin, and sat by Isabel's closed door.

When Bentley reached the deck, he found that the work of destruction was even more rapid than he had feared. The men were working cheerily at the boats, and had rigged a couple of small tackles, which assisted materially. Bentley joined them, and, with willing hands, and words of sailor comfort and encouragement, put new life into the undaunted, though weary seamen. Upon inquiry, he learned that Coffin had detailed the people for their stations—the second mate and four of the crew being ordered to go in the whaleboat, and the rest in the large life-boat with himself. As the former was lowered to the water and manned, Coffin cried,—

"Now Niles, don't forget, when you get clear

of the ship, pull dead to leeward, and, if you land, wave a lantern; there's one stowed there, in the stern sheets."

At this moment, a wave struck the ship, and lifted the boat almost even with the rail; as it was falling into the trough, a sharp knife severed the line which held it, but not before a figure, unrecognized by any one, was seen to leap from the bulwarks. Who it was, no one could tell in the darkness. As the next sea caught the surging boat upon the upward curve, it rose again, but, almost at the mizzen rigging, and, then, as if by enchantment, rushed into the gloom and was gone.

It was now after three o'clock, and the heavens were as black, and the gale blew as hard as at midnight, but the wind was steadier, and had shifted more off shore. When Bentley again climbed the rigging, he saw, in the west, one faint, tremulous star, and, as he gazed intently through the darkness, he made out, astern, the blackness of a bulk, of a rounded mass, which was different, in a faint degree, to the flat background of gloomy sky; and, once, when the roar of gale and sea were stilled for an instant, he heard the echoing boom of waves beating somewhere upon a hard barrier of sandy beach. As he came out of the rigging, Coffin was awaiting him.

"I believe there's land of some sort astern; I thought, too, I saw a high sand-hill, but it may have been my imagination."

"Where away was it?" asked Coffin.

"All around the ship, astern—the hill broad off the starboard quarter."

"Well, we will pull for it," Coffin replied. "And, I say, Colonel, as the boat is nearly ready, will you bring the others."

Bentley entered the cabin, and called to Lorrimore. He waited a moment, and, receiving no answer, called again. But Lorrimore had disappeared, and, as he turned impatiently to Isabel's room, the door was quickly opened and closed. As she came toward him, Isabel hesitated, crossed to her father's door, and, standing there for a moment, lifted her hands, as if in an agony of supplication.

She was closely veiled, and wrapped in a hooded water-proof, and as Bentley took her hand it was icy-cold, and to his words of endearment she could trust herself to give no answer. Her head was bent, her veil was tightly drawn, and, as they struggled through the water surging upon the decks, she trembled with an emotion which made her almost helpless. The sea had subsided a little to leeward, and the staunch boat, by careful management, rode safely alongside. Willing hands lowered Isabel from the rail, but, as Bentley was about to follow, he stopped, and, with a sudden fear, exclaimed,—

"Where is Lorrimore?"

There was no answer at first, and then, the sailor who had cut the bow-line of the whale-boat, said he had seen Lorrimore swinging himself into the second mate's boat, just as it shoved clear of the ship.

"Are you sure?" asked Bentley,—"sure it was Mr. Lorrimore?—for this desertion would be murder."

"Yes, sir," asserted the man, "the gentleman, he come aft on a run, grabbed the painter, and, as he jumped, sir, landed all in a heap in the fore sheets, sir."

The rest of the crew took their places, Coffin, last of all, and, when the boat rose upon the next wave, the line was cut, ready oars pulled clear of the vessel, and, as the long swell swept onward, the frail craft was folded in the arms of the angry night. As it fell into the hollow, abreast of the mizzen chains, Bentley thought he heard a human voice crying for help. But he reasoned he must be mistaken, for there was no one left on board, and Lorrimore had clearly betrayed his trust, at a moment when a craven only would have thought of himself.

Steadily and surely, the men pulled to leeward, the undaunted Coffin grasping his steering oar with the sweep and grip he had learned in his whaling days. The waves were black and silent, though at times, a crest, suddenly bitten by the wind, would curl viciously into the boat, and blind the rowers with spray.

At first, Coffin steered by the star, which shone brightly in the west, but he soon shouted with his old-time chuckle,—

"It's all right, lads; there's the shore, and Niles is waving his lantern. Cheerily now, it's only a long pull and a strong one, and we'll land the lady yet."

Bentley had spoken no word to the grief-stricken woman beside him, nor had she voiced a fear, or shown her sore distress. He had watched with eager eyes, thinking only of her safety, the darkened wall ahead, and, when he saw, searing like lines of fire, the crescent of white beach and the circling sweep of the lantern, he put his arm about her and whispered that the crisis had come. Tightening the straps of her life-preserver, he said, tenderly,—

"Remember, cling to me; we will live or die together."

She did not answer, but, with bent head, leaned upon the gunwale, as if saying a prayer.

The narrow crescent broadened into a curve of foam and billow, and the roar of the surf echoed seaward, with the thunderous reverberations of storm-clouds penned in resounding hills.

"Steadily, lads, steadily," cried Coffin, quickly, but with no tremor in his tone. "Mind your oars, there, for'ad. Steadily, my sons, and stand by to back, when I pass the word."

A mighty wave, hungry for the beach, lifted the boat on its unbroken crest, lapped it joyously, sang of the rest and peace ahead, lured it swiftly and surely shoreward, and then with cruel sport would have dashed it upon the beach, had not Coffin checked its onward rush, as the billow's crown became a dark and broken hollow and its base a cataract of foam and sand. But there could be no hesitation now, and, with a last cheery word of comfort, the boat dashed landward upon the incoming wave, steered straight to the point where the rope-joined lines of rescuers stood almost in the tumble of breakers and the drag of undertow to receive them.

In clarion voice, which rang as a bugle above the bursting sea, Coffin cried,—

"Stand by! now lads—jump." As the crew sprang clear, the steering oar broke like a sapless reed dried in winter's frost, the comb of the wave turned the bow to the left and upward, and as the receding water rushed brokenly seaward, the boat capsized and its hapless occupants were struggling with the unreasoning instinct of self-preservation in the surf.

All save Bentley and Coffin; and when their rescuers afterward looked at them lying on the shore, they saw the wrists of the two insensible men were red and bleeding with salt-steeped wounds, for the nails of the woman had clung as acid bites and scars.

Upon recovering consciousness, Bentley found himself lying upon a ridge of sand which crowned the isthmus. He was powerless to move, though as the flooding blood came back to heart and brain, his first thought was of the woman he loved.

He heard the voices of the fishermen dragging further up the beach the life-boat taken by right of might from the locked doors of the deserted station; he saw the moving figures of men, and, as he looked upward, he beheld a waning moon shining through a rent veil of ragged clouds, the light of many stars, and, to the northward, the flying masses of scud and storm bank; above all, he heard the measured beating of the breakers, and the long and sibilant swish of the undertow, dragging seaward the waters which tried impotently to clasp the land they had sought with such longing.

Presently strange faces, but friendly ones, bent over him, and one was kneeling by Coffin, chaffing his hands and forcing between his teeth a draught of spirit. When Bentley's strength came back, he lifted himself, and saw just beyond the fluttering dress and cloak of a woman.

He could not stand as yet, but, with desperate effort, crawled painfully to the place, and took the white, cold hands in his. That she was not dead, the moanings which rose and fell with every slow breath told, and he thanked God, even for this. The crescent moon sailed like a fairy shallop into a silvery sea, and, as the waves of light flooded the glistening sand, Bentley saw on the pale forehead a long, deep cut, from which the blood was trickling. He raised her head with a touch as gentle as a woman's, and turning the face to the moonlight, tenderly lifted the blood-sodden veil from the wound which the keel of the overturned boat had given.

The cool air lingered lovingly upon the lips and eyes, and, as these moved feebly, the flooding glory of the night filled her face,—and he saw not Isabel,—but Lorrimore.

"Lorrimore?" Bentley muttered wildly,—"Lorrimore? what can this be!" And then rising on his knees and bending over the dying man clad in woman's guise, he cried in anguish,—

"Tell me, for God's sake, Lorrimore—speak, man—tell me, where is Isabel Marsden?"

The pallid face flushed, the burning eyes turned to the ship and the sea that was rending it, and the wan lips murmured faintly,—

"There! In the Halcyon's cabin, strapped to her bed, and, God forgive me, I have done it."

"In the Halcyon's cabin," shrieked Bentley, "and left by you to die. Then go to the hell which waits you."

His grasp tightened about the throat of the dying man as he bent his knee upon the heaving breast; but the tired hands faltered, his eyes saw only the blackness of a new despair, and, as the gray dawn was breaking, Clifford Bentley fell insensible by the side of the wretch he had almost died to save.

CHAPTER XI.

DAWN.

THE cool air revived Bentley, and staggering to his feet he found that the day had dawned. He looked about in a stupor, and, as the broad beams warmed into blue the gray of the upper sky and the breakers caught a golden radiance as they rolled landward over the shallows, he saw the Halcyon, not a mile from shore, still opposing her bruised body to the sea.

The mizzen mast alone was standing, and not only were the bow timbers gone, but almost to the waist the frames stood with wide separations, which showed that the ship was fast going to pieces. Though the gale had blown out, and the fresh breeze which succeeded had not added to the size of the billows, the wind was still strong enough to keep the sea in angry motion.

There was not a moment to be lost, and, with the strength of desperation, Bentley staggered to the beach where the fishermen were wheeling the life-boat to the station. "Keep fast the boat," he called to them, "for Heaven's sake, keep fast."

His hearers waited in wonder, as, panting for breath and hoarse with excitement, Bentley stood before them.

"In that ship," he cried, "bound to the bulkheads and left to die by a murderer, is a woman,—is Miss Marsden. Dead or alive, we must find her. Who will go with me?"

Who?—all!

The sea-bruised crew, the hardy fishermen, man and boy, strong and weak,—not one faltered. Even the dead awoke to life, it seemed, in the hope of sharing in such a deed, for, most pleading of all, one voice sobbed,—

"Beyond any of them, and first, take me." It was the haggard face of Waite. "Take me," he repeated, in the incoherency of his clouded mind. Niles came to his old commander, and said,—

"Not yet Captain, but by and by; you must sleep now."

"Yes, you are right," Waite answered, "but, remember, I was the last to leave my ship. I had to spring from the bulwarks to do it, but I was the last, as the captain should be."

It was he, who, rushing in delirium from his hiding place, had been taken for Lorrimore.

Selecting the sturdiest of the volunteers, the boat was manned, and, with a veteran surfman at the steering-oar, sent safely seaward. Its fight was a rough one,—a struggle of brawn and brain, of muscle and heart, but it was sure.

Stroke by stroke the boat climbed the billows, flashing on their spray-lipped crests, hidden in their sombre hollows,—but always onward. The measured strokes rang in rhythm, the blades dipped deep, rose high, and gleamed with diamond clusters, and the steering-oar, leaving a serpent's trail in the water, held, with steady course, the shining bow straight for the stranded vessel. The crescent of the shore faded into a fringe of foam, the sand beach narrowed into a silver line, and, at last, the Halcyon, agleam in the sunlight, showed what the gale had done.

Her bow pointed at an angle off shore, the sudden shifting of the helm to escape just as the breakers were seen, having turned her nearly eight points from the course she had been steering. As the life-boat entered the pool of wreckage, it was hauled alongside to leeward by a trailing halliard, and, when it reached a place amidships, where the bulwarks were carried away close to the deck, Bentley and two of the crew jumped, as the boat rose, into the water still flooding the lee gangway.

Bentley entered the cabin alone.

All the doors were open save one, and, as he slowly pushed this back, he saw, lying on the bed, the unconscious figure of Isabel.

Was she alive or dead?

In her pallor, in the untrembling lips, in the stilled breathing, it seemed to be death. The hair hung in clusters about her face, and upon her motionless bosom rested the rounded plug which Lorrimore had fashioned so quietly. It was bitten and ragged with splinters, and the strings were wet, and red with blood; the bleeding corners of the mouth, the bruised and torn skin, and the purple indentations in her cheek and neck, showed where the twine which held it had been tied and twisted.

Calling the two fishermen, Bentley cut the cords which bound Isabel, and, then, as the dead are carried, they bore her to the bulwarks, where the boat, into which they lowered her, was waiting.

Bentley stood for a moment in silence, and then said, resolutely,—

"My lads, there is one other duty to perform. Come with me."

They entered the dismantled cabin, and wrapping Marsden's body in the linen of the bed, brought it to the boat, and placed it by the side of the daughter he had loved so well.

"Let them not be divided in death," Bentley whispered,—"if death it be."

Dropping clear of the Halcyon, the boat swept shoreward, and, as Bentley turned for a last look at the ship which had brought him so much pain and joy, a wave, mightier than its fellows, burst through the weakened frames and rushed aft with terrible force. As it receded, he saw the mizzenmast, freed from its stays and shrouds, reel from side to side, and, with a sudden cant to leeward, plunge overboard, carrying with it, or smashing in the fall, the cabin he had left a moment before.

When the draught which Bentley forced between the purple lips of Isabel warmed the fluttering heart, he detected the faintest thread of pulse; and, as they neared the shore, a faint glow suffused her finger-tips, the lips trembled with the thrill of reviving animation, and the eyelids twitched nervously under the steady glare of the sun.

Landing beyond the heavier breakers, in a little bight behind a hillock of sand, which, further out, curved, like a sickle, into an angry barrier of shoal, they carried the still unconscious girl to the hut furthest from the station, and, upon the ridge where Bentley had been placed, they laid the body of Marsden. Next to him, by a grim chance, was the upturned face of Lorrimore, stilled now to all fear, for in the companionship of the solved mystery there was no dread for either.

The unsparing labors of the fisherman's wife fanned the dull ember into a gentle flame of life, and, at last, when Isabel opened her eyes, remembrance dawned, and, though her voice refused to utter the words she wished to speak, her eyes gleamed with a desire of questioning, that was sad in its impotency.

"There, there, deary, try and sleep," said Mrs. Winston, "everything is right; they are all saved—all, except four of the poor sailors."

The woman soothed her with words of homely comfort, and as Isabel turned to the window, where the sunshine brought into fantastic light and shadow the rude timbers of the room, she saw the bright sky, the turbulent sea, the silvered sand, the moving figures,—and Bentley. Then she closed her eyes, and, overcome with fatigue and excitement, fell into a restless slumber, that was filled with dreams of winds, and waves, and death.

Bentley sat with bowed head at the door of the hut until Mrs. Winston said the crisis was over; then he stole quietly up the beach, and, falling upon his knees behind a sand dune, offered a thanksgiving for the mercy which was greater than the sparing of his own life.

As he looked about him, while he rested until his emotions were under control, he saw for miles and miles a sandy isthmus, flanked by outlying islands and inner sounds, and broken by scattered clumps of trees, patches of scrub and wide areas of stunted woodlands. Everywhere were the hard beaches, the clusters of sand, the shallow inlets, and the sea. To the southward a conspicuous hill arose, and, beyond, long stretches of bald beaches glistened on barren wastes; to the westward was a wooded island fringed by marsh and shoaling water, which the tides joined by slues and sedgy inlets, and framing all were the blue hills of the broken mainland.

For miles the shore was littered with wreckage, and in the distant waves derelict spars and timbers were taking the glistening sunlight on their sides. This was the shore of North Carolina, as he had learned, and the hill was Nag's Head, the dreariest and saddest of all the places which await mariners upon our long stretch of southern coast-line.

When Bentley came to the fishermen and sailors, unconscious of the loving and grateful eyes looking out at him from the hut, he saw that the bodies had been gathered in one spot. Winston said,—

"Five in all, Colonel, not countin' him as we uns brought ashore. Hadn't we better bury them?" he added, pointing to a little enclosure back of the shore, where in a rude cemetery the dead and often nameless sailors cast up by the sea were laid to rest within touch of its spray and breeze.

"Yes, and this one first," answered Bentley, indicating Lorrimore; "let us pity him who failed to pity us."

"Hadn't my wife better look out for her," suggested Winston, who had heard the story imperfectly.

"No, he is a man dressed as a woman, and God forgive him for some wicked purposes of his own."

Coffin had recovered his strength and was devoting himself to Captain Waite, who clung to the mate as a child does to its mother. Niles and some of the crew were busy making rude tallies by which the dead could be recognized hereafter, and the carpenter and the others were fashioning rough boxes for the bodies.

Bentley took his old place for a moment outside of Isabel's door, and when he learned she was sleeping easily, followed the men who were carrying the dead to the God's acre beyond. As he stood on the ridge looking at the crumbling wreck of the Halcyon, Winston came to him hurriedly, and said,—

" Colonel, if my wife can be spared from the young lady, she had better go over to the cemetery and look out for the one you told we uns to bury first."

" Your wife! Why?"

"Well it's more her business than mine,—more natural like."

"More her business than yours?" inquired Bentley, wondering at this strange persistency.

" Yes, Colonel, that 'ere man *is* a woman, after all."

CHAPTER XII.

DAYLIGHT.

TWO days afterward Isabel was carried to the mainland, and in a fortnight she was able to sit upon the wide veranda of a hospitable manor house, watching the gulls circling in the Sounds and the fish leaping from the shining waters. Health and strength came so slowly that the benumbed mental processes took up lazily their old orbits of action; and for long hours of the perfect days she would try with vain endeavor to put together, piece by piece, the facts which made the mosaic of these later days of trial.

She could recall nothing of her rescue, nor of the first shock of the wreck, for with sad iteration her memory ebbed and flowed about the misery of her father's death and the horror of the crime which had left her to die alone in the stranded vessel. Beyond these two truths, all else was formless and dim in the mist of dreams.

With the vivifying balsam of piny autumn woods and of salt winds transmuted in the alembic of barrier trees, health breathed upon her, and little by little, in responsive gratitude for nights of restful sleep and days of peaceful idleness, the mind awakened to a clearer knowledge of the past.

Bentley had secured quarters in a farmhouse near the shore, and day by day brought her the simple gossip of those honest people, and, with every tender device love could invent, sought to lead her, by quiet roads, into the lands of happiness she had known of old. He never spoke of the wreck, nor of her peril, but of the days when first they met.

In October, when the blue hills of the old North State were bright with the gold and ruby of the leaves, and the cool, star-gemmed nights gave a more cheerful glow to the pine-knots crackling on the flaming hearths, she made Bentley tell all he knew of her father's death, and of the scenes that followed. As he finished, she said, with tear-filled eyes,—

"And it was you who saved me, and my dreams were true?"

He lifted her white, blue-veined hand, and kissing it, answered,—

"No; it was the inscrutable wisdom of God which wrought the miracle."

As soon as she was strong enough for the

journey, they went, one day, to the fatal isthmus across the Sounds of Croatan and Roanoke. Of the Halcyon, not a timber was left, but of the gale—who will ever measure the agony of the bruised lives, or the gratitude the rescued felt for what these hardy fisher people had done.

Isabel went to the cemetery alone, and when Bentley joined her, he found the graves strewn with the wild flowers she had brought; and, on those of Marsden and of Lorrimore, alike, rested the crosses of golden-rod she had wrought with such loving care.

In after-days, Bentley told her, that of all the gracious deeds in her life, none could equal this.

That night, as they watched the sparkling logs, and heard the mutterings of a rising gale, she revealed the mystery of her last hours on shipboard.

After Bentley left her, she had fallen wearily upon the bed, mindless of peril, and conscious only of her father's death. Finally, recalling her promise, she was about to rise, when she heard her door quickly closed and bolted. A firm grasp and a cruel blow forced her upon the bed, and, in a moment, two quick turns of a thick cord lashed her helplessly to the framework of the berth. She tried to free herself, but a noose, deftly slipped over her hands, drew them, extended, to the headboard, and, as she screamed for help, a little rounded plug, with a breathing-space bored in its centre, was pushed into her mouth, and by the quick strain of looped strings was twisted and tied back of her head, and around her neck and arms.

She was bound and gagged.

It was a devilish deed, performed neatly, and with the despatch and skill such as sailors and surgeons alone possess.

In the darkness, she could see that a man was putting on her dress and cloak, and, then, the stillness of the room was broken by a voice, which she recognized as Lorrimore's. He seemed to be insane, and with a fierce exultation which, in the days of convalescence even, rang in her ears with portents of awful evil to come, cried,—

"So—at last! at last!—and after all this waiting! Do you know me? I am Marion Darlington, the woman whose life you wrecked. I have followed you with patient waiting, ready for any desperate chance, and fate has given it'at last. I have you now, so sure, that the angels of Heaven cannot save you. As Philip Catlin died, so shall you die; as my love was taken from me, so shall yours be lost to you. Once, in the first madness of despair, I tried to kill myself, but the woman whom I saw go to her awful death, filled me with horror, and I fled, only to plan and plan, through sleepless nights, how I might reach you.

"There lies the dead body of the man who spurned me for you; he wanted you only for himself in life, and he shall have you in death. And such a death!—almost as sad and hopeless, as my poor life has been. Outside, with no thought but of you, is the man who would save you at the peril of his life—he, *he*, will rescue me, and leave you to a fate none will know in all time. Should I reach the shore alive, who will tell that I came in your disguise, when, in a moment,—where the night is dark, and the current strong—these clothes, cast to the sea, will leave Lorrimore saved, and Isabel Marsden gone, as if she had never been. Listen!—do you hear him—it is Bentley, calling for Lorrimore, and awaiting you. Ah! how you would sue for pity, could you speak. But did he who is dead —did any one pity me? No!—and now I shall leave you with the sea, that pities none;—leave you dying with your dead, and to the mercy I have always known."

Isabel remembered but little more. After the first agony of fear had passed, she freed her lips, by a supreme effort, from the plug, and screamed for help, but when this was unanswered, she fell into a stupor which trembled for hours on the borderlands of eternity. It was the echo of this pitiful cry which Bentley heard, as he bent to soothe the shrinking form beside him in the boat. And she who heard it, in joy, knew not that it was the voice of her sister, calling as one deserted in the wilderness.

In the spring Isabel and Bentley were married, but not until Marsden had been laid at rest in the peaceful cemetery of the village from which he had departed with boyish ambition to make the world his own. Catlin, too, was buried in his old home, just outside the circle where rest those who died for their country during the great war in which he had done his part so well.

To that distant home in California, Bentley accompanied the body of the poor girl whose life had been without savor and grace; and as it was laid, with prayers and tears from friends of old, by the side of the mother, whose only fault it was to have loved so blindly, no one save the priest knew, that beneath the stone which marked the resting-place of Maria del Gado slept she who had been called Marion Darlington.

But as the twilight lay like a benediction upon the quaint cemetery, a bronzed and bearded gentleman knelt in the sanctified ground and placed upon the fresh earth a wreath of immortelles in memory of the love that Pedro de Saldo cherished for the unwedded bride of his youth.

Bentley found awaiting him upon his return two letters; one from Coffin inviting him to the launching of the new Halcyon, of which he was to be the master, and promising that he would get a rare welcome from Captain Waite, who had given up the sea and was too hard at work selling fish and lumber to bother his brain with cobwebs and spun-yarn-twistings about spirits.

The other letter was from Girard.

It began with many felicitations after the French official manner, and was most formal and precise until it reached the pith of the story where it warmed into a friendly blaze of semi-professional confidence. It told in detail the search for Camille Desmoulins, and how, at last, the mystery had been solved by the confession of an attendant at the Morgue, whom Girard had hunted down. Hoffman, sparing neither time nor money in the search, one day recalled old Mother Blinder, the chiffoniére, who had reared the missing woman.

"So, so," said the hag in her hovel on Montmartre, "that pretty butterfly is gone. Where is my amber heart then? the one I gave her, and which was blessed by the Pope. Ha! ha! my braves, that was a rare joke, but she believed me, and she swore never to give it up. Find that, and there you will see my sainted child."

The attendant at the Morgue had been arrested upon a petty charge, and in his pocket the amber amulet was found. He finally confessed that he had taken it from the body of a woman, in whose dress he had slipped a handkerchief belonging to an American lady.

"What was the bribe? Twenty napoleons.

"And her other instructions? That he should do this whenever a body so disfigured as to be unrecognizable should be found.

"What was the name upon the handkerchief? Marion Darlington, he recalled it, though foreign, because he had been paid to inform a gentleman who lived in the Rue Chaillot when such a corpse was brought from the river.

"The name of this gentleman? M. Clifford Bentley; and in proof he submitted the address in his memorandum book. We have sent the scoundrel to Cayenne, and Hoffman has erected over the grave you bought a monument to the memory of *cette chère* Camille, to the woman who killed herself in a drunken frenzy which she called love.

"And the other—the Madame Darlington; she, surely, if alive, is plotting harm, but who can tell when or where it will strike—or, by my faith,

—why? For there, even we, who live in mysteries, fail."

* * * * * * *

And so, silently and irresistibly, rule fate and chance, and thus surely do our deeds decree, not always the roads we travel, but the goals we reach at last. Fate and Chance men call them, but with what different meanings. Not for him is their truth made plain who holds that humanity evolves only in predetermined mode, nor for him who denies that chance is aught but the effect of a cause unknown. For Fate and Chance are what we make them, and to each of us is every thought or action sure to bring a certain loss or gain.

Of the dead, pity Marion Darlington above all; for in the unfolding light of immortality she spoke those repentant words which saved the tender woman who placed upon the grave of the sister she knew not, the cross of charity and of love.

THE END.

www.ingramcontent.com/pod-product-compliance
Lightning Source LLC
Chambersburg PA
CBHW021807230426

43669CB00008B/658